Love, Life, Quirks, and Quarks

Love, Life, Quirks, and Quarks

A Family History

The history and analysis of the MacNaughton, McArthur, Curtis, Silver, Vasilevsky, Loftus, Bradford, and Bunyan Families

MARJORIE J. MCARTHUR

Charleston, SC
www.PalmettoPublishing.com

Love, Life, Quirks, and Quarks
Copyright © 2021 by Marjorie J. McArthur

All rights reserved
No portion of this book may be reproduced, stored in a retrieval system, or transmitted in any form by any means–electronic, mechanical, photocopy, recording, or other–except for brief quotations in printed reviews, without prior permission of the author.

First Edition

ISBN: 978-1-64990-495-9

DEDICATION

This book is dedicated to the women of my family from the "greatest generation":

My mother Caroline MacNaughton, a natural leader, a civil and political activist, an artist, a fashion enthusiast, and a non-stop hard worker.

My mother's younger sister, my adorable 4'8", 89 pound, Aunt Alice Silver, who loved entertaining with family (many times in her garage), gardening and reading. I was never happier than when I was in her company.

My mother's sister-in-law Bernadine Curtis, an incredible soprano singer with a charismatic temperament.

My father's sister-in-law, Thelma MacNaughton, as good-hearted as they come, a generous philanthropist for the down-trodden, who taught her four kids to do the same.

My father's other sister-in-law, Dr. Elizabeth MacNaughton (Aunt Tiz), very accomplished, as you will see in the book, mostly in education and politics, and the funniest of the group.

Why am I dedicating this book to these 5 women? Because of the efforts and sacrifices they made to keep our various families and generations together. Thinking of the family first, not themselves, they arranged many family road trips and vacation spots.

I. INTRODUCTION

We are a mix of Yankees, Southerners, Westerners and Canadians with many interests, some of which may be considered quirky, and many professions, some notable but all important (e.g., engineering, physics, chemistry, biology, professors and teachers, CPAs, law, aviation, musicians, information management, creating databases, dance, sports, technical and creative writing, medical doctors and technicians, dental hygienists, literature, plumbing, farming, theology, philosophy, executive management…and loving life). The direct line of Margie's and Peter's (Margie's husband) is a diverse group of Scottish, British, Irish, German, Scandinavian, Iberian Peninsula ancestry, all related to Northern Europe, and came to the US and Canada relatively recently.

II. MARGIE'S GRANDFATHER NORMAN MacNAUGHTON, GRANDMOTHER KATHLEEN CHALK MacNAUGHTON, FATHER WILLIAM MacNAUGHTON and his TWO BROTHERS, DOUG and JOHN MacNAUGHTON

Bill (Margie's father), brothers John, and Doug

My dad's generation of the MacNaughtons began with the birth of three boys of high character and born closely together. Bill and John, the middle and youngest, respectively, were born in Vancouver; the oldest, Doug, was born in in New Haven,

Connecticut, when their parents, Norman and Kathleen, lived there while Norman attended divinity school at Yale. Norman and Kathleen were both Canadian and of Scottish/English/Irish descent. The men in that generation wasted no time getting PhDs. Norman had two, in philosophy and theology, the latter being an honorary degree as he wrote his thesis on a rather ambitious topic, "Why Is There Evil?" I presume he came to the conclusion that this question could not be answered by a mere mortal, so he got up one evening and calmly tossed his thesis into his burning fireplace. John earned two PhDs as well.

Margie's paternal grandfather, Norman MacNaughton

Norman preached regularly on Sundays without pay, so even though they had little money (the small amount their sons brought in from paper routes and washing dishes), but the family always lived in a comfortable Methodist parsonage while the boys were growing up. As my dad, Bill, put it, "We were poor, but we had status." Armed with degrees in chemistry (Doug and Bill) and psychology and industrial psychology (John), they were ready for scholarships to the grad school of their choice. *But wait.* Bill had a plan. Her name was Caroline Curtis, an elementary school teacher from Alpena, Michigan, who, ironically, at the time was dating Bill's older brother Doug. Bill came and snatched her away much to everyone's surprise.

III. MARGIE'S MOTHER, CAROLINE CURTIS MacNAUGHTON

Caroline Curtis, Margie's mother

My mother, Caroline, could only be characterized as constantly in motion, artistically talented, incurably optimistic, and incredibly organized. Perfect for my passive, studious dad. She loved embellishing stories to the point of many inaccuracies, even changed facts sometimes even within the same story. Of course, these inaccuracies were quickly pointed out by in my scientific family, but that did not stop her.

She was just being interesting and colorful, and that she was. Her Uncle Fred Smith who was a Circuit Judge in Alpena, MI, used to tell her she would never be seen as a credible witness on the stand in a courtroom.

To show how generous and creative she was, one spring when I was away college, she sent to my dorm at the University of Tennessee (UT) a homemade short-and-top outfit every day for two weeks (all hand sewn by her without patterns, her own design). While raising us in Kingsport, she was president of the Girl Scouts, the local Women's Symphony Committee and the Kingsport Youth Orchestra, the Girls' Club, the Republican Precinct of East Tennessee, the American Association of University Women (AAUW), and an officer in many other clubs and charities, like the Methodist Church Boards, Garden Club, and more. I suppose she could have run General Motors if it'd been in Tennessee. Oh, settle down, Michigan relatives! She could iron twenty of my dad's shirts, plant boxes of flowers, make two dresses from scratch, including ironing, and visit a sick neighbor before noon. I know a lot of this because when I was a teenager and slept until noon on weekends, she kindly recited all the jobs she had finished while I was sleeping. My dad never did this; all he could have said is, "I read a book or watched sports while working a jigsaw puzzle" (he didn't even look at the picture on the puzzle box to help him). My kids inherited this jigsaw puzzle talent. My dad's belief at the time was that men worked outside the home and women were in charge of the household, the children, school projects, meals, house and yard work, volunteer work for the community, and generally providing a quiet sanctuary when their husbands came home from work.

Then there is the matter of her cooking. First of all, she didn't like to eat; she could only eat meat if it was overcooked (*burned* is more like it), and she longed to be a vegetarian. Her spaghetti recipe consisted of Campbell's tomato soup, which she mixed into overcooked, limp pasta. The three spices she kept in her kitchen were nutmeg, cinnamon, and allspice. You guessed it: she was baker, not a cook, and a terrific one! She really knew how to make a pie crust, as her younger sister Alice did. Her blackberry and lemon meringue pies were amazing. She also specialized in ginger bread (Bob and I always argued about who got the most whipped cream; she finally started meticulously measuring it to shut us up) and delicious chocolate cookies with vanilla icing, smaller circles of chocolate icing, still smaller circles of vanilla again, topped with a chocolate candy. I wasn't much of a sugar or chocolate fan, but I was happy when I came home to these. I also *loved* her homemade angel food cake with caramel glaze and homemade whipped cream (I do not think she was aware of the canned type; after all, my dad and I did the grocery shopping). Too bad all her cookbooks disappeared after she died. So did many other things, typical of my non-materialistic dad; he just gave away my mother's things to the first person who showed interest. I asked him why he did that when I had agreed with Mother on which items I would enjoy. I know my sweet dad meant well; he just didn't have room in his brain for such trifles. Gone is most of her artwork, her piano, her sewing machine, her car, her good china, and sterling silver flatware with "Mc" engraved on each piece (could have been Grandma MacNaughton's). Especially important to me was a complete set of beautiful Christmas dishes, which I really wanted for my family, maybe because I love Christmas so much. I am sure that's due to my mother and Aunt Thelma. My mother turned our entire house into fairyland. Aunt Thelma always found the most creative gifts and was so fun, no matter where we were. She calmed me down while driving a snowy road to Tahoe *at night*. The Michigander softly said to the Southerner (me): "This is nothing." Aunt Thelma was excellent at any game one could think of, including bridge, my lifelong passion.

IV. THE MacNAUGHTON TENNESSEE CHRISTMAS

More about Christmas: While growing up, we kids, led by Jimmy, were driven to find out what the presents were under the tree on Christmas Eve. A creaky hallway led from all our

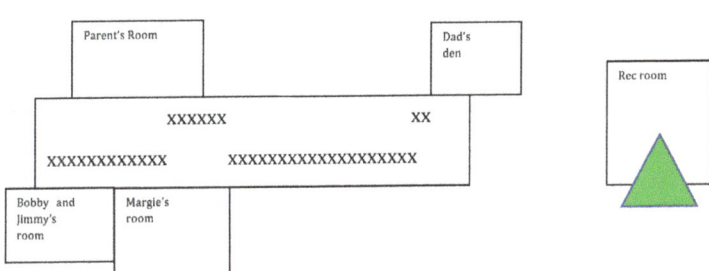

bedrooms to the rec room, where the tree was. The trick was to make it down the hallway without a sound so as to not wake up our parents. Prior to Christmas, when our parents were out playing bridge, we practiced tiptoeing from our bedrooms to the tree according to a predetermined route on the creaky hallway floor, mapped out by Jimmy (*quirk*), as shown above (*x*'s indicate creak points). The hardest part was opening and closing the hallway door knob without a sound. Our parents didn't want us to believe in Santa, as they didn't want to lie to us. We did previous research on the sound, lighting, and walking techniques that would not enter our parents' bedroom. We were most vulnerable by far when walking, dropping things, and we just didn't consider jumping up and down or running, no matter how excited we were. We took about three trips each Christmas for about four years until we were old enough to get wrapped presents.

V. THE MOVE FROM MICHIGAN TO TENNESSEE

My mother taught elementary education to put my dad through graduate school where he got his PhD in organic chemistry in 1942 at the University of Michigan. That same year, my parents had a baby named Jimmy and my dad got a good job offer from Tennessee Eastman Company located in Kingsport, Tennessee, without even applying! Its parent company, Eastman Kodak, is headquartered in Rochester, New York.

My dad, a young organic chemist

While my dad was not one to judge anything, other members of the family did. Many Michiganders said, 'You're moving to a small town I've never heard of, where? The hillbilly state of Tennessee? Jimmy would not have approved of moving from Michigan to Tennessee either, had he not been a baby. So off went Mother, Dad, and Baby Jimmy from Ann Arbor to a little city called Kingsport, Tennessee in the foothills of the Smoky Mountains not far from Davy Crockett country. Its population was around 15,500 in 1945, with about one-third of them working at the Eastman plant.

Tennessee Eastman Company was founded in 1920 by George Eastman, who also co-founded Eastman Kodak headquartered in Rochester, New York. Who would have imagined a company as big as Eastman Kodak would have a plant in Tennessee? Well, I would like to tell you. Kingsport being located in the foothills of the Smoky Mountains, where its forests had suitable amounts of wood to make wood alcohol (methanol), used in photo processing, and acetate which was used to make polymers. Other benefits in Tennessee: labor and land were cheap, and there is no state income tax. Not to mention the Tennessee Valley Authority (TVA), which flooded thousands of acres of farmland and built 20 dams for producing inexpensive and abundant hydroelectric power for the state of Tennessee and parts of neighboring states. Additional advantages were controlling the devastating floods in those same valleys. The TVA lakes were beautiful places to boat, water ski, fish, and have picnics. In 1942, as a government contractor, Tennessee

A FAMILY HISTORY

Eastman constructed Holston Ordinance Works to manufacture explosives during WW II. This is where my dad worked during the war.

So, who would work for a large plant in such a small city one might wonder. Well, the answer is quite interesting. Many of the residents were hand-selected, highly educated scientists and engineers from the best colleges in the United States, Canada, and Europe, mostly non-Southerners, as you might suspect. I am not sure of the size of Eastman when my dad started in 1945, but when I was in college and paid attention to such things, Eastman had seventeen thousand employees at the Kingsport site. By then, Kingsport had a population of about thirty thousand people. My dad was most proud that he had over one hundred PhDs working for him. We were lucky that we were surrounded by many small towns that provided hundreds of blue-collar workers.

Eastman had the best benefits: like generous paid vacations (six weeks per year for my dad after 35 years); a yearly wage dividend; movies, a pool, tennis courts and the Eastman cabin, which is on a large, beautiful property and hosts many Eastman and private events. On Saturday morning, they had an interactive live children's show called Horse Krickers, which the children loved. My dad was particularly attracted by the fully equipped photographic labs where he and I spent almost every Saturday developing his color pictures that he had taken with two Hasselblad and one Lindhoff high-end cameras. It soon became a costly lifelong hobby, as most of the pictures were taken during trips throughout the world. My dad loved exhibiting his best photographs internationally and giving them to friends and relatives. I still have hundreds of his photographs that are in great shape.

In October 1960, disaster struck. I was at my friend Donna's house up the street for an after-school club meeting. Boom! Boom! Boom! Donna's house shook. We ran outside and saw a huge mushroom cloud to the east. We guessed Washington, DC, had been hit by an atomic bomb! We ran inside and turned on the radio. There had been a huge explosion at the Eastman factory, specifically in the organic chemical division (my dad's division). I walked home pensively, scared to face my mother, sure that she would tell me my dad had died. I saw my mother and a neighbor in my backyard watching the cloud, not seeming upset. "Where's Daddy?" I asked. My mother said, "He left for South Carolina this morning." I felt a huge relief—I had forgotten he was traveling. When he was notified about the explosion he came home immediately and went straight to Eastman. He didn't come home for days. It turned out that sixteen people were killed and two hundred were injured. It was the Aniline plant that had exploded due to over-nitrification of benzene due to the failure of the nitrogen addition valve. Usif Haney, the plant manager, was among those killed. I was friends with his son Bruce. A sad day indeed.

My Dad didn't overlook giving us the best education, no matter the cost. My brother Bob is the only one who took him up on his unlimited offer to go to any school and stay as long as we'd like, getting as many degrees as we wanted.

Jimmy did take my dad up on part of his offer. My dad did contribute to Duke's tuition as Jimmy only had a partial scholarship for undergraduate school. He had 100 percent full scholarships throughout his post-graduate education. After Jimmy graduated from Duke University in 1964, he attended the Monterrey Language Institute where he became fluent in Russian. He became lifelong friends with Mrs. Elischer, the Hungarian woman who ran the school, and her family. Naturally, Jimmy took Hungarian classes and soon had better grammar than Mrs. Elischer, according to her. Our two families merged, and all became great friends. My dad pushed my brothers to get a PhD in Physics, but he did not push me. He pointed out that he wanted me to go to a good college where I would most likely, meet someone to marry. He overcame his double standard later when he learned about the Women's Lib movement, then promoted and became passionate about it. My dad was an extremely fair man.

I was offered a scholarship to get an advanced degree to teach botany at the University of Tennessee (UT) which I wanted to take advantage of. I was engaged at the time and my banker fiancée couldn't find a job in Knoxville so, I turned down the scholarship, got married and moved to Chattanooga. In 1970 I settled for a job as a biology lab supervisor, technician and release coordinator at Cutter labs starting at $400 a month. How many of you are cringing over this? Why didn't my fiancée get any kind of job in Knoxville until I finished graduate school? This should have been my first clue. I was beginning to hear about women's lib from a group called the National Organization of Women (NOW) and amazing women like Betty Friedan and Gloria Steinem and many more. It was time to have a talk with my dad.

My father and mother at Eastman event

Like most Eastman children, we enjoyed many perks. Eastman encouraged families to work for the company generation after generation. My dad found a job for me at the medical center after I graduated from UT with a degree in biology with a focus on microbiology. Even though it was a summer job, as I was getting married in the fall and moving to Chattanooga, I was allowed to shadow their microbiologist, who only worked in microbiology one day a week. Meanwhile, I helped in the medical lab, drawing blood and doing hearing and urine tests as well as whatever else was needed. One might question (as I was not a med tech) why I was drawing blood and probably some other tasks I was not qualified for. Requirements were probably looser back then. At any rate, I loved it and the staff I worked with; everyone was friendly.

VI. BACK IN TIME. WHEN MY BROTHERS WERE YOUNG

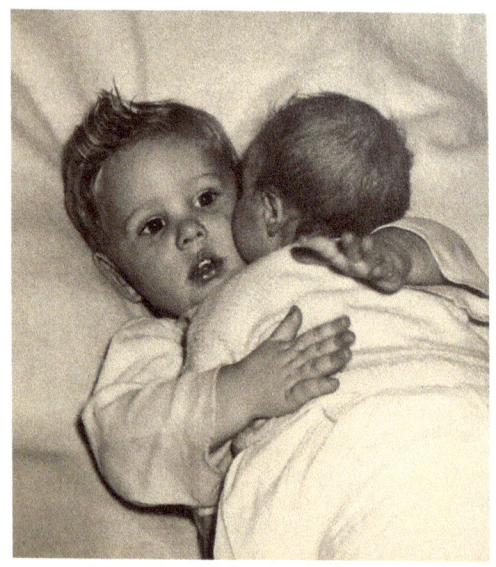

My brother Bob hugging his little sister

Back to 1945: My middle brother Bob was born, he was called the jackpot baby because he was so well behaved and was so cute with curly blond hair. By the time we lived in our first little house in Kingsport, Jimmy was proving himself to have quite an independent mind. He would not eat his meals unless they were delivered to his room by electric train (*quirk*). He would not go to bed one night until Dad came home from work and told him the Roman numeral for five thousand, which he could not find in his Dad's textbooks (*quirk*). Not something you'd expect from a three-year-old, but then again, he is seventy-eight now and still does unexpected things.

Jimmy was always experimenting and we were rarely informed of the goal of the experiment. For example, he dreamed up the bottle cap census (*quirk*). Jimmy, Bob and I spent a substantial part of our middle years collecting bottle caps. On a daily basis, we'd use a magnet tied on a long piece of string and drop it down into the bottle opener slot in the soft drink machines at various stores in Kingsport and during our travels. Our mother had no problem with us storing the caps in paper bags up in the attic. She also allowed us to line up the caps on the carpet so we could count and sort them for the yearly census. The last annual census showed 50,000 caps collected, Pepsi winning with the most bottle caps and Coca-Cola a strong second.

Since he was quite a bit older than me, Jimmy loved to sit with me and teach me some of his interests, which I still appreciate to this day. For example, he taught me about the solar system and the distance from the planets to the sun; Morse Code; how to play bridge (one of my passions to this day).

When my brothers and I were young we took many road trips in the summer with Mom and Dad to Michigan, Florida, Texas, Arizona, etc. Jimmy would sit in the front seat next to either Mom or Dad who was driving, with his finger on a map monitoring our progress. Mom made a soft flat area in the back of the station-wagon for me to play with dolls. Also in the back of the wagon Mom made neat folded piles of everyone's clothes for the trip (no suitcases, only a case for toiletries). And the piles were arranged chronologically so that the top of the pile was for the next day, and so on (*quirk*).

VIII. WORLD WAR II AND THE SILVERS

Aunt Alice and Uncle Jack (John D. Silver).
Jack was in the army during WWII.

Meanwhile, World War II had started. My mother's sister, Alice, moved in with us in Tennessee (1943), pregnant with her first child (Don) without her husband, Jack, who was serving overseas. He survived landing on Utah Beach on D-Day +1. His job was to collect the dead bodies and decontaminate the beach for the next wave of US soldiers. Alice gave birth to my cousin Don in the Kingsport hospital, a

In front of the Michigan stadium: Bill Crawforth, me, Carol, Bob, and Beth

fact Don rarely advertises! Alice and Jack later had two more kids, Dick and Beth, in Alpena, MI. Dick the middle child, is my age, with the signature Silver talents: charismatic and fun-loving ; he, like me, is also a biologist. He married Jane, and they had a dog named Spot (naturally). They have two great kids, Greg and Brian. The youngest of Alice's children, Beth, is every bit as fun and talented as her brothers and married a most interesting man named Bill Crawforth, a lawyer in Ann Arbor. Such a fun guy! He fits right in. Pete and I had a wild weekend with them in Nashville as well as in Cincinnati when Pete was building a plant there. We rented a house on a big golf course, and they nailed it. Beth often beats Bill at golf. Hee-hee!

Dick and Don are excellent golfers too. Beth and Bill are University of Michigan football fanatics, graduates and are part owners part owner of the Little House, a renovated garage adeptly made into a sports bar across the street from the

Big House (Michigan stadium). The Little House is the destination after (or during if it's cold out) the game, with TVs all over, theater-style chairs, hooch, warmth, and barbeque. Heaven! The Silver family is a house divided during football season, as four of my Alpena family went to Michigan State! Beth and Bill have a son, T. J., who is married to Libby, a talented hair stylist. T. J. is a packaging expert, embedding the labels with useful computerized data. They have two adorable girls, Emerson and Evelyn. They also live in Ann Arbor, to my cousin's delight. Enough about the Silvers for now. No, they are not Jewish. In fact, many of us have a long history with the Methodist Church, except for the infidels in Houston and Japan. What's more, my parents met at the Wesleyan Center at the University of Michigan.

VII. THE START OF THE JOHN MacNAUGHTON FAMILY

On December 7, 1941, my aunt Tiz (nee Elizabeth Hackett) was out teaching children on an Indian reservation, then on a date with a guy trying to win her hand, while John MacNaughton was in grad school. When she heard the breaking news of the Japanese bombings of our ships in Pearl Harbor, she got up from the dinner table, went to the phone in the hall, and phoned John saying she had decided to marry him on Christmas Day. Her mother had said no, but her father Norman said yes. They were married by Norman on December 25, 1941. They had two children, Ann and Phil, my cousins.

Since Ann and I were close to the same age, our parents decided we'd be best friends. It worked, maybe too well: we wrote to each other in code. She scared me with garfish in her backyard lake in SugarLand near Houston, and we made dinner every night…probably not too tasty, but Uncle John and Aunt Tiz never complained. Ann and I drank a little whiskey, complete with a fake hangover. We watered it down and blamed the maid (at least that was the plan). We shoplifted at the Galleria. We smoked in the doghouse; I thought Tiz was pretty cool when she caught us. We complained about Phil, the younger brother tagging along to the movies even though he was about as cute, nice, funny, and smart as they come (I told him when we were older that I think I look more like him than any other relatives; bless his heart: he considered it a compliment). Ann and my only genetic similarity turns out to be our large boobs (undoubtably from Grandma MacNaughton), which we figured out in Eleuthera in the Bahamas while enjoying a picnic lunch. Ann and Tiz came from Houston that morning for the picnic and then turned around that afternoon and went back to Houston for no good reason (*quirk*). My hilarious Aunt Tiz pointed out, "This is the farthest I've ever come for lunch." It was twelve hundred miles.

Our parents allowed Ann and me to visit each other in Houston and in Kingsport every other summer. I wonder if our brothers were jealous. After all our mothers were strong, competent extroverts, and our dads were more passive regarding home matters. My dad bought me a doll from every business trip, and the boys never got anything. I had a lot of dolls. I joined the Houston MacNaughtons on a vacation road trip from Houston to Canada to Kingsport. It was a blast being in the car with John, Tiz, Phil, Ann, and me playing and singing along with our ukuleles. John loved to sing "Camp Granada" (with his beautiful voice). Tiz and Phil would tease each other in the cutest way. For example, when we were stuck in a traffic jam, Tiz asked Phil (maybe ten years old) to get out and talk to the driver three cars up and tell her to get off the road (*quirk*). Bill and John's children are Canadian citizens, as their dads were born in British Columbia. Ann, Phil, and Jimmy have gotten their

Canadian passports. Jimmy even renounced his US citizenship. I'm working on mine.

In Indiana, at Aunt Tiz's birthplace, we found out why Tiz is so witty. Her whole family is. The three sisters were sewing, and one of Tiz's sisters kept sticking pins all the way into her bra without flinching. We finally found out she was wearing a falsie. Tiz was well known in Texas politics. Ross Perot chose her to be on his Select Committee on Public Education (SCOPE). Tiz was the only one without a private plane. In fact, Ross called Tiz and asked her to meet him at six o'clock the next morning (he was in Dallas, she in Houston). There was Ross Perot at 6:00 a.m. in front of her office. He asked her to be on the committee, and a lovely friendship developed. SCOPE continued for months and made many decisions to improve high school education in Texas, most notably the no pass/no play policy regarding athletics.

On a Colorado vacation in Estes Park, Ann and I showed off our limber backs on the jungle gym. We hung out with a cute boy about our age; I think we were both jealous of each other. Phil has two lovely children with Vickie: his son, Christopher, and his daughter, Jessica. Christopher married Tiffany DeBellefeuille; they now live in the Netherlands and have three small children. Phil is a lawyer in Houston, as was Ann. Aunt Tiz achieved a doctorate in education and was quite well known for her positions on the Texas Board of Education and her political contributions. Not only was she well read, but she also made Ann, Phil, and me read for an hour every day. Ann and Phil were whizzes, but I was slow as molasses at reading (I am sorry I did not keep this up when I returned to Tennessee). This is a fabulous idea for a parent to insist on reading time as soon their small children can read through higher school. Ann and Phil are incredibly well-informed, articulate adults. In 1950 Uncle John started up and was chair of the first Industrial Psychology Department at the University of Houston, and later, fittingly, John was buried under a tree on campus.

Family lunch in Texas: Geoff, Ann, Pete, Aunt Tiz, Phil's son Chris, Phil, Margie, and Bob

We have been fortunate enough to get together with Phil as adults. Peter and I enjoyed our fast-paced dinner at Hobby airport, and especially when he came to our clubhouse in Rossmoor, a fifty-five-plus community in California where we now live. He has a solid pro-fracking argument that I bought into completely. Phil is very convincing; I'd hate to meet him on opposing sides of a courtroom (just as I would hate to meet Ann under those circumstances). I remember when we had some sort of legal problem and Phil offered his help for free. Somehow the problem resolved itself. I forgot what the issue was. I also appreciated the legal advice that Phil gave me when my brother Bob died suddenly of a heart attack at 69. It was right in line with Bob's girlfriend, Jill's, opinion. I sensed that Bob would want their opinions honored. Jill went on to be the executor of the will, and she did an outstanding, efficient job.

Phil married Jeanling on Valentine's Day in 2019. Jeanling was born in 1988 and grew up in Guangzhou (previously anglicized as "Canton") in a multilingual household (Cantonese, Mandarin, a grandmother and aunts who spoke so-called regional dialects that were actually independent languages, English at school starting in elementary grades). Independent and adventurous, Jeanling has visited (by herself) twenty-two countries. After operating two hotels in Guangzhou, she decided to go to business school, heading first for France (cheaper), here she learned French and then came to the United States (stronger reputation). Phil and Jeanling share a love of travel and made it to Hawaii before the novel 2020 coronavirus shut things down. During the pandemic, Phil and Jeanling are hanging out with their two dogs, two cats, and two parrots.

VIII. THE DOUG MacNAUGHTON FAMILY, maybe the CLEVEREST and QUIRKIEST OF ALL

Our young Bill MacNaughton family were lucky in that we traveled, mostly in the United States and Canada, but mainly to see our relatives or just go to Florida so Dad, Bob, and I could dive through huge waves on the Atlantic side. Jimmy was the navigator on our car trips, who tirelessly followed along with his finger moving on the map following the trip. We stopped to take a picture of every US and state road sign. Jimmy carefully placed the pictures in the correct order into a photo album, which nobody looked at except Jimmy. Did I mention that he memorized the whole Greyhound bus schedule, a book about five inches thick? We made trips to Ohio, Michigan, and Canada frequently to visit Uncle Doug, Aunt Thelma, and their children.

My dad talked Uncle Doug out of graduate school in chemistry, and thus he graduated from Yale Divinity School like his dad. Uncle Doug became a minister in various communities in the Midwest before returning to his alma mater, Adrian, as a professor. He was kind and interesting and drove my dad crazy with his shortcuts and frequently getting lost on our road trips. Jimmy loved Doug's trips. Jimmy even returned from Duke, his undergraduate school, to Kingsport by way of compass—no state or US highways allowed (*quirk*). The normal three-hour trip took nine hours. Mother was driving, and I was a passenger; we were very patient with him. If my dad had been with us, the compass system would not have been implemented. (Note: This was the same weekend I got kicked off the majorette team for missing a parade. I'm still bitter about that.)

Uncle Doug inspired me to write this book because he had written a similar family history, which I treasure. It seems we are too young to ask questions about relatives we don't remember, are far away, not available or gone. Uncle Doug's wife was Thelma. Her father was a doctor in Georgia, so she was the sole Southerner in a Yankee family (until my family moved to Tennessee). Thelma was very giving and honest to the nth degree, if you can handle real honesty, that is. My son, Steve, loved her because in Lake Tahoe, everybody was mad at Steve because he was mean to Nicole, except Aunt Thelma. She took Steve under her wing, taught him games, and made him feel special the whole trip: a lesson for all of us. Years later when Thelma was terminally ill, he sent the sweetest note expressing to her how much her love and attention meant to him. This shows how long even kids remember kindness and how important it is to their upbringing.

Thelma and Doug had four kids. George, the oldest, is the perfect oldest brother: he is smart, well behaved, quirky in a delightful way, unique, fun, and generous. He got an

MBA from Boston University and married a lovely woman named Deborah Warren. Deborah is from Boston and has two kids from a previous marriage, Kristin and Nicholas Robbins. They have six kids of their own spanning four decades: Honor (a physician), Colin, Fiona (a mother), Sam, Domino, Piers, and Cecchi. Speaking of Cecchi, he and his siblings and uncles have played a game called crokinole (similar to shuffleboard or curling) for many years, which they still play (*quirk*). They go to the crokinole world championship in Tavistock, Ontario. The first year that Cecchi went, at age seven, he was world champ for his age category! All the MacNaughtons that are George's immediate family are Bostonians (some have been strewn out since growing up). His family has houses in Andover, Nahant, and a farmhouse in Vermont. Pete and I visited them in Nahant, a wealthy island northeast of Boston. The house is on the Atlantic Ocean; we got a workout just walking down the driveway. George was busy matching his kitchen drawers to his house in Andover, so that all utensils were in the same order (*quirk*). I questioned the sanity of this. They had never stayed overnight in the house that we were visiting in Nahant (*quirk*).

Here is a story George told me: in early June 1965, George borrowed his dad's old Raleigh three-speed bicycle to ride from Albion (at the end of his sophomore year of college) to Lake George in upstate New York to a boy's camp, where he spent thirteen summers as a counselor. As a precaution against flat tires, he strapped his unicycle to the back luggage rack of the Raleigh and took off, heading east through Ontario. The trip took the better part of a week, and he has no memory of camping out each night, but he must have done so at the side of the road, except the night with cottage friends (Thelma had a cottage in Thornbury on the Georgian Bay, Ontario) who plucked him from the side of the road and took him to their home for the night. I think Thelma must have warned them to be on the lookout for her son George. He did need that unicycle, for after riding on Ontario's dirt roads for hours, the rear hub froze with sand. So he put the Raleigh and other gear on his shoulder and road the unicycle to the nearest town. The proprietor of the local gas station gave the Raleigh a thorough cleaning and tune-up (*quirk*). He spent an hour riding his unicycle around the gas pumps giving the local kids rides. About four years later, while a student at Boston U, where he earned his master of divinity degree, a roommate and George rode their bikes from Boston to San Francisco in late May and early June.

After several years of teaching elementary school math, Deborah pointed out that they could not live on teachers' salaries, given the number of children they were raising. So George chose business school over law and earned an MBA from Babson College and then went to work for Eastern Uniform Company in the early 1980s and stayed there for twenty years, eventually becoming president of the company.

A FAMILY HISTORY

Aunt Thelma and Uncle Doug's second son, Tom, is a carrot head; he married a lovely young lady named Cristine and made their home in Adrian, MI. Tom is quite the long-distance runner. Jean and John are the twins and youngest. They both are single and work at the local theater. Jean also works at local bookstore. John and Tom both ride a unicycle too (*quirk*). John is active with the Dominican nuns. My husband, Pete, noticed at Thelma's funeral that they hugged John so affectionately. When I asked why, John said, "The nuns *love* a good funeral." Uncle Doug was buried under a tree on the Adrian campus (similar to his brother John, who was buried under a tree at the University of Houston).

Aunt Thelma and Uncle Doug's brood: Christine (Tom's wife), Jean; next three, George and Deborah's children (names must be guessed from the nine names given on page __); Tom; John; four more of George and Deborah's children with more names to be guessed, the prolific George and Deborah; Margie and Pete standing supervising and hungry

*My Aunt Thelma and me at her cabin in
the Georgian Bay, Ontario, Canada*

Our family visited them at their cabin many times on the Georgian Bay in Ontario.

My cousins would dive right in the cold water, but not the female Tennessee MacNaughtons. Our Tennessee waterskiing lake was a little less than body temperature in the summer; even then it took Mother and me a good half hour to get in the warm water for skiing.

Uncle Doug was given the Adrian College President's Medal after he retired, just the third such honor given out in that college's history. Our family was honored when one of the main campus buildings at Adrian was renamed MacNaughton Hall in honor of Grandpa Norman and Uncle Doug.

OUTSTANDING ALUMNI AWARD

A. Douglas MacNaughton '34 is professor-emeritus of religion and philosophy at Adrian College. After earning his bachelor degree in chemistry from Adrian College, he received his M.S. in chemistry from the University of Michigan, his B.D. in religion in higher education from Yale and his Ph.D. in church history from The University of Chicago.

Doug has been a member of the Adrian College community for most of his life. He taught at the College from 1961 to 1983, serving on numerous committees and on the Alumni Board of Directors. He is currently completing a history of Adrian College.

Uncle Doug receiving his professor emeritus award, Adrian College

Pete and I at Adrian College: Plaque commemorating Grandpa MacNaughton and Uncle Doug

IX. BACK TO THE SILVERS

We visited the Silvers and they us many times. We'd always get excited when visits were coming up. From my point of view, it would be hard to beat the fun we had. Uncle Jack would grab me laughing when we drove up the driveway and off; we'd go to do our spectacular gymnastics. He was strong and tall, and I was little and limber; we thought we were something. I wasn't nearly as little as my adorable Aunt Alice, who was four-feet-ten, and if she jumped on the scales just right, she weighed one hundred pounds. We loved their house, which didn't look interesting at first, but it was. I now appreciate the advantage Aunt Alice had being married to a plumber. There was a basement downstairs where Uncle Jack kept his huge supply of tools and machinery. He enjoyed making thatched chairs, but there were always too many orders to keep up with. As busy as he was, he always made you feel special. Lucky for us Jack's son Dick inherited his skills, especially in making exquisite furniture. Uncle Jack played the trombone for the Alpena City Orchestra. Aunt Alice was a wonderful cook and kept her freezer and various fruits and vegetables in the basement.

On the Silvers' main floor was everything else: three bedrooms, two baths, a kitchen, and a living room. Jack had figured out a way to get warm steam into the master bath in the morning. Luckily, Beth and Bill managed to keep that house after Alice and Jack died. I'm probably not doing it justice, as it is hard to explain; nonetheless, it's the most comfortable place that I've ever been. Maybe has something to do with its occupants.

One of our craziest times with Don that stands out is Bimini in the Bahamas close to Miami. My college roommate Andy (female and our sorority president) and I flew to Bimini and had nice place to stay (a woman my mother knew ran it). All the rest of the guys, Cousin Don, a Michigan State football player friend, a veterinarian friend, my fiancé, and a male Tennessee cheerleader came the next day—*the perfect storm*. Andy's real name is Andrea; she is from Long Island, and her dad was a brain surgeon in Manhattan. Her mother was a cool Southerner who hosted spring break for us the previous year, and we had a terrific time. Andy and I went directly to the bar beside our hotel and started drinking Yellow Birds, which involved rum and something yellow and singing the so-titled song.

We were flirting with the nice-looking guy next to us naturally. He was there for big game fishing on a neighboring island. For no good reason, I started singing my high school song ("Here's to dear old Kingsport High School…"). The man next to us sang along. Huh? You should have seen my face. He was John Palmer, who was working for the *TODAY Show* as the newscaster at NBC, part of his forty years there. He graduated with my brother Jimmy from Dobyns-Bennett High School. The Kingsport Library was named after the Palmer family.

The group of us were quite good at beach pyramids. That night we all went to a dance shed, and it turns out Adam Clayton Powell was there; as you may or may not know, he was the first black congressman to serve the United States (Harlem). He was deported to Bimini on corruption charges. As I was sitting next to Don listening to the music, another black guy came and asked me to dance. I said, "No." Don said, "Why don't you dance with him?" I could not believe what came out of my mouth! "Because he's black." I then realized I may have had racist tendencies, which certainly didn't come from my family or friends. I was shocked at myself. Don didn't waste time giving me a good talking-to: "All the beautiful blond girls at MSU hang all over the black football players." "Really?" I said. After all, we only had one black player (the first one ever) on the Tennessee Volunteers team, and there were no white girls anywhere near him. I let go of any racist tendencies then and there and

From left: Don's friend Mike Clift (a UT cheerleader), Andy Rhodes, Don's other friend, and Whitey

was so glad I did. Don is so sick of me telling this story. I still have a little bigotry left: we skiers and fishermen never got along when on Boone Lake in Tennessee, as they got very mad at us for disturbing the fish and their lines. Yes, I know it was the spoiled college kids' fault, since we intimidated them. They even shot at one my friends one time!

We ran out of money. All I had was one of the service station cards that occasionally lets you eat at a random buffet. So we ate coconuts until it was time to leave. It got worse. Andy and I went to the Delta desk in Miami and were told our flights were canceled. What? Andy had one dime, and I had that rarely useful credit card: we were pretty sure we were screwed. Unbelievably, Andy got paged just after we left the Delta agent; Unbelievably, just seconds after we left the agent, Andy was paged. The MSU football player wanted to know if we would like a ride to Knoxville. Did we ever! They met up with some other Spartans, so we were quite crowded in the car. I lay flat on the top of the back-seaters, and off we went. Near the Georgia border we spied a buffet. *Yes! It took my credit card.* You can imagine how hungry we were after three days of coconuts. I was a little worried about Mother not being pleased with me feeding the bunch; then I remembered Don, who could do no wrong in Mother's eyes. I was protected! No meal ever tasted better, even to the Yankees. The Yankees let us off in Knoxville, and off to Michigan they went.

X. GORDON and BERNADINE CURTIS FAMILY, MOTHER AND ALICE'S OLDER BROTHER

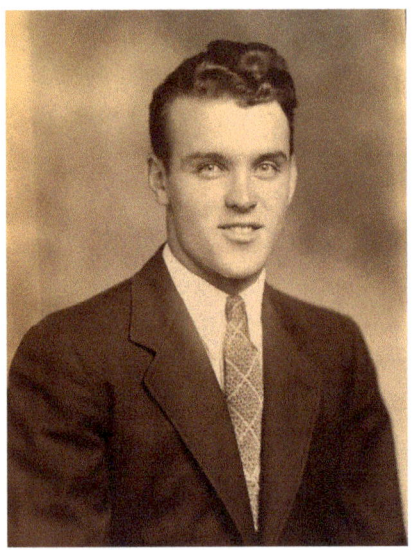

My mother's oldest brother, Uncle Gordon, father of Gordon and Clarkc

My mother's and Alice's older brother Gordon was very handsome. Mother said in school, girls would make friends with her just so they could meet him. He became a manager and worked for Cummins Engine Company in Columbus, Indiana. He married my Aunt Bernadine who could sing beautifully. They had two boys, Gordon and Clark. Both graduated from Indiana State. Gordon is a masterful trumpet player, the only professional musician in our family. He has played the trumpet for over 50 years. He played lead trumpet for Bob Hope, Ella Fitzgerald (the nicest lady he ever met), Vic Damone, Kenny Rogers, Goldie Hawn, Gladys Knight, Doc Severson, Al Hirt, to name a few. He routinely played in Las Vegas on New Year's Eve. He invited us many times, but I regret that we never went (I blame the kids). Clark was an announcer for TV news, car racing, etc. He and his wife, Yvonne, a hair stylist, are fond of their 3 dogs and 3 cats, all rescues. Clark is an a most talented Christmas card writer, like my daughter Nicole's husband, Aran. Oh, how I wish those two would send me frequent letters! Clark is passionate about Eastern European politics and spends time there helping his political friend. Clark and his wife and pet clan live in Charlotte, North Carolina.

Cousin Beth, Margie, and cousin Clark Curtis

XI. BOB, JIMMY, AND MARGIE MACNAUGHTON GROWING UP

Bob was best in the jump-around in the state of Tennessee in the trick and slalom in the early 1970s.

Growing up with my brothers, Bob and Jimmy, was interesting to say the least! Bob and I were very close once we got beyond the childhood squabbles. Apparently, I said to him when I was in junior high, "Why don't we just be nice to each other." That was it; we were as close as could be for life. Life isn't so difficult, is it? Bob was the state of Tennessee's best all-around water skier, and I won some gymnastic medals in state meets. Good thing we were both short and stocky (actually, I was only short); we both had good balance, as did my mother, who was an ice skater.

My mother could slalom water ski into her sixties (in the Caribbean, a native commented that he had never seen an ancient slalom before). Bob and I were close enough in age (two years) that our friends were each other's friends around high school and after. Bob went to so many universities that he almost always was assured of having a winning team on college football days (Northwestern, Washington, Florida, and Tennessee, where he got his PhD in inorganic chemistry; he also essentially got a PhD in solid state physics at Florida as well, as he passed his final comps, but didn't pick up the degree. His reason: "I don't like physics") (*quirk*). I got Bob a T-shirt that read, "Dangerously Overeducated." If you want a good trivia team, it's best to have Bob and Pete's sister, Laurie, and her well-read husband, Zack. Bob and I remained close in our adult years. Once while visiting me, Bob decided that I would waterski the length of my apartment's pool (*quirk*). Several fellows were holding the rope and running as fast as they could; we did it.

Bob's jobs were related to computer chips mostly, firms like Texas Instruments and AMD. (Husband Pete McArthur notes: I find it interesting that both Bob and Margie got a good education that led right into two new industries destined to boom, electronics and biotechnology, respectively. I

LOVE, LIFE, QUIRKS, AND QUARKS

Pulling a rope connected to Margie waterskiing in a pool

Our beloved TenneSea Breeze, a forty-foot motor yacht, which we bought in 2005 and lived on for a few years. Those years included my recovery from pancreatic cancer and Pete's recovery from heart valve surgery.

went into biotechnology too.) He managed to have homes mostly at different times in Houston, Dallas, and his beloved Austin…and, of course, a ski boat and a big boat (OK, a yacht). Soon he got his marine captain's license.

A big coincidence: Pete got a dream job offer in San Diego the summer of 2005. Bob got a job offer in San Diego in the summer of 2006. Margie's company, Genentech, decided to buy a plant in San Diego, which would begin preparing for the FDA licensing inspection the summer of 2006. And guess who my boss recommended for the job? So the three of us moved to San Diego. After I convinced Pete to buy a boat (not just a boat but a small yacht!), in one of the boating capitals of the world, the three of us lived aboard our two boats. Our boat, TennesSea Breeze, became one of Pete and my best memories ever. We had her docked at the Marriott Marina and loved to go enjoy live rock music and the Tiki bar on weekends at the Marriott. We also had access to a well-equipped fitness center. We had great time boating to Catalina a few times: "Twenty-six miles across the sea, sunny Catalina is waiting for me." I sang this many times on my uke, which I still have. One of our best memories is going whale watching outside San Diego harbor. We were told that a young whale was near shore, confused as to it's position. We were told to not get closer than 100 feet, but we still had a great view of the whale swimming with dolphins accompaning. Then, amazingly, one of the dolphins came up to our boat and jumped toward the bridge, clearly telling us to stay away from and protect his friend the whale.

TennesSea Breeze was even more important to us when Pete and I had major surgery (Pete, heart valve replacement; and me, Whipple surgery for pancreatic cancer). We feel that the boat helped us heal; the soothing environment on the water; the gentle swaying with the tides; and the friendly people on the dock.

XII. MEETING JILL

The Silver family and friends at Long Lake. Front: Margie, Beth. Back: Son, Michael; Alice; Nick's wife, Libby; Nick, Marijean, Don, Fred Boyton and girlfriend, Pete, Bob, and Dick.

When we met Bob's new girlfriend, Jill, as they arrived for our Alpena family get together at 11:00 p.m. at Long Lake, Michigan, I was enchanted. How perfect, I thought: she is funny, smart (retired vet professor at LSU), kind, interesting, and full of adventure. Bob had met his match in Jill. She even won the national "Distinguished Educator Award" shortly after they met. In the three years they had together before my beloved brother died of heart failure, they shared many Mardi Gras beads, danced and danced, found a northern passage in Minnesota or something like that, were both foodies, enjoyed the best of cuisines and beer, except for the French Laundry in Yountville, which Bob, Pete, Jill, and I didn't even try to get in, as it was chosen the best restaurant in the world by Michelin a couple a of years ago. Reservations were virtually impossible, and if you do get in, the cost is at least $2,000 per couple. (We did forage their gardens, though.) My son Steve, who was working with restaurants to set up their software at the time, met their head chef and owner, the famous Thomas Keller, a few times and was invited to a lunch for two. He turned it down, and I was furious!

When the backyard flooded at Jill's Baton Rouge house, for Jill and Bob it was kayak time; they did it in the gully. Jill's worst fault is that you can't keep up with her. As an example of her energy, she and her three sons designed and literally built their Baton Rouge house from the ground up. Jill and Bob volunteered frequently at the Super Bowl, Mardi Gras, and charitable events. They were even extras in *Bonnie and Clyde*, but they didn't make the cut. Oh, I wish they'd gotten married.

XIII. MARGIE'S FIRST WEDDING

*Whitey and I on a cruise in the Caribbean.
Pete loves Margie in this picture!*

I did have a brief first marriage with a fun fraternity guy at UT named Whitey (Eugene White). I had lots of good (and questionable) reasons for getting married so young—for example, all my friends were doing it, and my materialistic little self wanted the wedding presents that my engaged friends had, which were artistically arranged on tableclothed display tables: sparkling sets of china, coffee cups, various glasses, gleaming silverware, serving pieces, linens, etc. I went to work for Cutter Labs in Chattanooga, and he worked for a local bank. One day I came home and told him excitedly that we were being transferred to Berkeley. His response: "I could never leave the South." I'm starting to see your point, Michiganders. I told my mother I was moving to California and leaving my husband behind. She said she was always worried about my marrying a Southerner. I said, "I am a Southerner!" She said, "Not really." Hmm.

About this time I talked to my Dad about women's lib. But it turned out, because Eastman was progressive about equal opportunity, my Dad had already been educated in it. And I thought this was a time of true cultural change.

XIV. MY SECOND HUSBAND PETER

My second husband, Peter (now known as ex-Peter) was an optometrist and an expert bridge player. On our first date, I told him my parents just got back from Czechoslovakia on a photography tour (the company was called "Through the Lens Tours", as they specialized in going to the most photogenic places in the world). It turns out that Peter was born there (today, it's Slovakia). To my surprise, my mother loved the tours, which is difficult to understand, as photographers are patient; neither Mother nor I have ever developed that skill. My dad said patience can be learned; I don't think so. I didn't enjoy so much of my vacation time waiting for a sunset to be in its best colors or a midnight flower to bloom (called a night-blooming cereus, for you, Jill, in case you're going to Florida). Back to ex-Peter: The Slovakian connection caught my attention; plus he was an expert bridge player, a game I enjoyed. When I met him at the Watergate Apartments in Emeryville, California, we did play bridge together, although I wasn't in his league, but I learned a lot and really enjoyed the competition (current husband Peter McArthur note: Margie is a very accomplished bridge player and was patient enough to teach me the basics; it entertains her to this day.) His mother, Anna (we called her the Mutterchen), smuggled him into Germany. It helped that they had fair skin and hair and blue eyes, and both his parents were good-looking. His parents worked in a German hospital until after the war when they moved to Belgium. Finally, when Peter was nine, they got passage to the United States. He didn't speak a word of English but was fluent in Ukrainian (his dad's home country), German, Russian, and French; nonetheless, he was sent to an American school. His father, Vasily Vasilevsky, died of heart issues when Peter was in college. Mutterchen remarried a wonderful man, Vasil Klymuk, also Ukrainian. He was director of the Ukrainian Orthodox Choir in New Haven with Mutterchen as his soprano soloist. He was a joy to all our lives. He's an example of someone who lived a horrible young life; his twin sisters were torn from his arms by the Nazis, never to be seen again, and he was put in a concentration camp, although he was not Jewish. Yet in spite of these experiences, he was a wonderful grandfather to my kids and father-in-law to me.

Two of my favorite Mutterchen stories:

One time she was at the market asking the butcher for a specific cut of meat. He said, "You can't do that." She said, "Yes I can; *I am butcher.*" She had lots of arguments with various butchers—always winning, of course.

Another time, my girlfriend brought over a fancy pasta-making machine for Mutterchen to use. Mutterchen took one look at it and defiantly said, "All I need is a bowl and a wooden spoon." She must have forgotten about the rolling pin she used to roll out the pasta: "Thin like paper." Oh, yes, and the very sharp knife she used to cut the pasta shapes. She sharpened that knife before each use with one of those foot-long, tapered metal knife sharpeners that I think are impossible to use. She was scary fast with it, quickly moving back and forth, changing sides of the sharpener in the same rhythm of the knife with its sharp edge always touching the tapered metal.

She was a wonderful cook and taught me a lot. I had to watch, estimate amounts, and write them down. It was all in her head. "How much flour can an egg take?" One of my favorite recipes from her is *Fletchi s'apostoy* (pasta checks with cabbage). There is no such thing as spelling in the Czech language, so pronounce the words phonetically.

Recipe
1 head cabbage
1 onion, diced
3 pc bacon, fried and broken into pieces
Splash of vinegar
Make pasta checks: put 2/3 cup flour in food processor ("That's how much flour an egg can take").
1 egg
1T water
1t oil

Pulse till it forms a ball; roll out till thin like paper. Cut into checks (squares). Boil till pasta comes to the top (won't take long). Drain and rinse. Put shredded cabbage with a little bacon grease in a very hot pan. Stir constantly until it is very brown. Add onion pieces and bacon and cook just till onion is soft. Add splash of vinegar and pasta checks, pepper, stir, and serve.

XV. THEN COMES OUR THREE KIDS: NICOLE, MICHAEL, AND STEVE

Margie; my ex-husband, Peter Vasilevsky; his mother; and our kids, Moraga, California

We searched for housing and finally found a nice house in Moraga, California, a safe, vacation-like town with good schools supposedly (never mind that we sent all three of our kids to private schools with amazing results). After only one year of marriage, we had three peas in a pod (well, almost). Nicole, the oldest by two minutes; Michael, the comedian; and then Steve two years later. A funny story. When I brought Steve home from the hospital, little Mike and Nicole took inventory of the baby: "Baby has mouth, baby has nose, baby has eyes, baby has ears, *baby need teeth, baby need hair!*" All engaging personalities, smart children who have become amazing adults…although the teenage years were a bit challenging. Steve gets most of the credit for that. Nicole, a competitive ballerina, is an energy ball who loves academia. She graduated from Reed College on time (which is a rarity, as it is a difficult school). Reed is Aunt Tiz's favorite college. Today she holds a PhD in molecular and

Nicole was a competitive ballerina in the Bay Area.

cell biology and is married to the world's most interesting guy, Aran, a CPA from Fairbanks, Alaska. The happy couple live in Portland, Oregon, and their spoiled Devon Rex named Sapphire (a curly haired cat, tiny and playful…who still looks and acts like a kitten at seventeen). Odin, of the same breed, was Nicole's first purchase with her own money: $400. They love to travel worldwide and are crushed trips are being canceled due the novel 2020 coronavirus currently threatening us.

My oldest son, Michael

Michael is a good all-around popular guy who is good at everything he does. Much to his chagrin, he was his school's valedictorian (he didn't want to give a speech). He majored in physics at Colorado University and now works in the pharmaceutical business (like Pete and me). He has worked in Saigon, a city he loves, and now is working remotely while living in Columbia. I called him the comedian because when he was two, he made Nicole and me laugh pretending to be a mime. It was a short-lived career, though; he never did it again and doesn't remember it. We'll have to get it out of him someday. But he does still play the guitar, which he's good at.

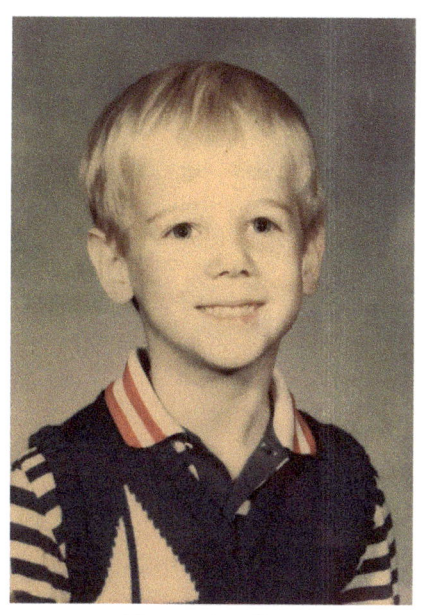

My youngest son, Steve

Steve, the youngest, is so adorable as well as competent. He is really fit and loves to work out with a perfect body shape. He is an independent thinker and is very logical. He saves his money to travel worldwide as often as he can. He lives in the area, so he visits frequently. I have Parkinson's, and there are many things that are challenging, such as walking, typing, or texting, writing by hand, cooking, etc. Steve is talented at math, computers, and languages. Steve is head of IT for the Bay Area Girl Scouts. I even enjoy talking to him about politics; I can't tell you how much this means to me.

XVI. POLITICS AND THE REAL WORLD

Growing up in my family, we talked about politics frequently (except Jimmy, who had no interest in it). My brilliant dad loved to explain how my mother turned him into a Republican, using arguments like allowing the people to run the government that serves us, keeping it small and useful for mainly administrative work and security for the people. He noted how incompetent the government is, partially because it's almost impossible to fire people, particularly minorities, and government officials generally have no experience making money by running a business; it's all given to them as taxes. I've seen many examples of this working so closely with FDA in biotech site audits and later for well-known ex-FDAers on consulting projects. Even the good ones couldn't execute a chicken. After all, no one in the FDA has ever produced a batch of drugs. A large majority of former FDA employees (usually the cream of the crop, highly intelligent people) who transfer to the industry are not capable of successfully manufacturing or even testing drug products. The only job I've seen them succeed at is preparing for an FDA investigation or certain training classes. Some are good at conducting internal and external audits. Under no circumstances should you let them write a standard operating procedure (SOP), or you'll end up with a complicated, lengthy, and useless diatribe that includes every possible error that could be made and what to do about it. It would be too complicated to learn and would take forever to implement. The secret is to keep procedures simple with a separate SOP for handling errors.

My dad, who was raised by an academic, liberal, and socialist family, explained that living on a college campus was not living in the real world. My father simply said, "Socialism sounds good, but doesn't work." My father was in control of a huge budget[1], sold organic chemicals worldwide, and managed real people with a wide span of educational levels: the real world in a capitalistic society. In spite of my Dad's comment, I believe teaching is one of the most noble (and underpaid) professions that exist. My mother was a teacher and we have many great teacher/professors in our family. My friend John Cherry said that we think in generalizations, which is fine as long as we recognize the exceptions. Brilliant.

---

1 A little aside on what it means to control a huge corporate budget: It requires forecasting and written, approved annual goals and periodic checkpoints. Three basic categories make up such a manufacturing budget: 1) raw materials and supplies, 2) labor, which includes salaries, benefits, shift premiums, overtime, and consultant fees, and 3) overhead costs, such as facility leases, utilities, equipment depreciation, janitorial services, maintenance, training, safety programs, travel, etc. Also, the manager has to base the budget on data from marketing and sales as to projected sales forecasts. Pete found that when planning a new facility, he often cut the market forecasts for new products by half for designing the startup capacity while allowing for expansion in the future.

XVII. MY HUSBAND PETER

My husband-to-be was a hardworking, well-educated chemical engineer (MS from Stanford) who built the first stand-alone biotechnology plant in the world for Cetus Corporation, now Novartis, in Emeryville, California. Cetus produced the second biotech drug ever licensed for human use by the FDA, interferon beta, which is used to treat relapsing/remitting multiple sclerosis (yes, Marijean Silver has used it) and hepatitis C. I'm sure that Marijean remembers that interferon beta is intrinsically pyrogenic, which means you have a fever for two day after a single dose. I was a systems-oriented sass whose job it was to find observable weaknesses in Pete's facilities. But he's such a good engineer that I never found any serious issues in any of his new facilities. In case you're interested, the first licensed biotech drug was human insulin, manufactured by Lilly in a renovated facility in Indianapolis, Indiana.

Pete was the project manager for several new and renovated pharma and biotech facilities for seven different domestic and international companies. He designed and built another new facility in Emeryville for the commercial biotech drugs like interleukin-2. He upgraded the flu facility in Siena, Italy, which used chicken eggs to grow the flu vaccine. He upgraded a fermentation facility in Emeryville,

California, and Amsterdam, the Netherlands. He upgraded purification and aseptic processing facilities in Emeryville, California, and Puerto Rico. He designed, developed, and performed life-cycle validation on a new medical device, an implantable osmotic pump for Johnson & Johnson in Palo Alto, California. Next, he designed a dry powder inhaler device and scaled up production for Dey Laboratories in Napa, California, and Crailsheim, Germany. Over 5 years, in 3 phases, he designed and built a new $850 million manufacturing plant for Amylin Pharmaceuticals in Cincinnati, Ohio, to produce a novel combination dry powder drug and diluent in a dual chamber cartridge, which when mixed before use and injected to treat type 2 diabetes using a twice-weekly injection. Pete wasn't just a project manager; he was in management most of his career with his own staff and departmental goals and responsibilities to achieve. His highest title was VP of engineering.

XVIII: MARGIE'S CAREER

My first career involved dance, acrobatics, tap, jazz, and a little ballet, beginning as a student teacher in our local dance studio in high school. Luckily for me, my teacher, a former Rockette, opened up a dance studio in Knoxville. As I was attending college in Knoxville, I worked for her teaching dance. After college, I moved to Chattanooga. I became a coach/performer for gymnastics team. I only competed in two meets, district and Tennessee state, where I received silver and bronze medals, respectively.

I was in quality assurance, manufacturing, and compliance positions for five different pharma/biotech companies. I have supervised a biology lab in Tennessee at a time when we had four patient deaths due to contaminated IV solutions. The plant, named Cutter Laboratories (later Bayer), was shut down for a year and a half while becoming compliant with our regulations called current good manufacturing practices (cGMPs). All of our IV solutions were recalled and destroyed (several thousand). The reason(s) for the contaminations was never determined, but many, the FDA included, believe that our food-grade steam sterilizer was submerging the lowest sterilizer rack in water, not allowing the steam to reach the bottles of solution on this rack.

In the Chattanooga IV solution plant, I was supervisor of the biology lab and release coordinator (the person who reviews testing and documents prior to product release to the hospitals). I had a close friend, John Cherry; we were stuck in the plant until midnight, working with the FDA. We heard there was flooding outside but brushed that off. Our plan was to go see our friend and colleague to catch him up on the latest. On the street to his house (which I affectionately called, "the hovel"), we saw water of unknown depths ahead of us. John and I parked the car and hiked down the railroad tracks (me in high heels) singing, "I gotta brand new pair of roller skates" at the top of our lungs. Why I remember this, I don't know. We made it to our friend's house, talked for hours, and made his wife mad. We did that often; I mean, John did that often (OK, me too).

John was leaving soon for North Carolina, where he would help start up the largest blood fractionation plant in the world, and he asked me to join the effort. I was given a project by one of the VPs in Germany. They *love* documentation, and my friend and I had a few ideas. The blood fractionation process was two weeks long and complicated with hundreds of steps. The traditional way to document this process was on a double-sided one-page card. They recorded a temperature, pH, date, and operator's initials, and not much else. The Germans and the FDA weren't happy with such incomplete record keeping. They wanted to be able to reconstruct the whole process in case of a problem before product release or before needing an investigation. So I built a book: all the product-related procedures on the left and corresponding data on the right. This allowed us to delete hundreds of procedures, and the operators had the step-by-step procedure right in front of them to avoid mistakes, since they no longer had to go to a dusty shelf to look something up, which they did rarely anyway.

After I finished the BPR (Batch Production Record) project in Berkeley and trained technical writers from Chattanooga and Utah to write and install the BPR system in their plants, I became a real Bayer Berkeley employee, working in the documentation department. While I was on the project, I was working directly for the VP of manufacturing from Germany. I believe that's why it was successful. Now I was a lowly technical writer, but with good connections.

One of those connections, Dr. Paul Chin, transferred to Cetus, Emeryville, California, the first start-up biotech company (Genentech claims they were the first also; it depends on how you measure it, so they both are right). He wanted me to write and install the BPR system, manage the microbiology lab, and release the product. This was exciting to me as I was interested in learning the all-new, first-time-ever process. So off I went. After I'd been at Cetus for a few years, I got a call from a former employee of mine at Cetus who asked if I would be interested in straightening out the poor documentation department at Chiron, a newer start-up, also located in Emeryville, CA. I spent several challenging years at Chiron, learning more about management, and rising to Director of GMP Systems. Later I joined Abgenix, then Genentech for a few years and retired in 2008.

XIX. PETER'S FAMILY FROM L.A.

Pete grew up in Arcadia, California, just east of Los Angeles. After he graduated high school, the family moved to Ojai, California, known for upscale shops, beautiful horses, and riding trails. It was also known as Shangri-la in an old Hollywood movie, and for a well-known tennis tournament and excellent golf club. A number of Hollywood types lived there. His paternal grandfather and two great uncles, all three MDs, moved from Toronto to downtown LA to practice. Those were the days of house calls and physically going to traffic accidents. Pete's dad, Pete Sr., grew up under well-off circumstances, with servants and all. He immediately fell in love just seeing Pete's mother, Shirley Hanawalt, on campus. This is understandable; she is gorgeous! They both graduated from Stanford University; she had a BA in English, and he was a petroleum engineering graduate. They married in 1941. Shirley was an amazing homemaker and later became a teacher of the hearing impaired. Pete Sr. worked in engineering and construction sales.

They had four kids. Linda was profoundly deaf, but Shirley taught her and the youngest, Leslie, who was also partially deaf, to read lips, resulting in two highly functioning girls. Linda is an accomplished athlete, despite the fact she is my height (five-feet-two, in case you didn't know). She specialized in long jump, volleyball and golf. Frank Sinatra sponsored her trip to the deaf Olympics. She also has four master's degrees from hearing colleges and was head of IT for Honeywell and the state of Texas. She and her late husband, Don, lived outside Austin, Texas.

The third youngest is Laurie. She has three smart, fun, good-looking kids and one adorable grandson. Laurie is an amazing math professor and writer. She sends the best gifts! Big boxes full of gifts, all special. She and her husband, Zack, a professor and department head of English, live in Chico, California. Currently Zack has graciously agreed to teach us some Shakespeare, which we are loving; he's a great teacher. Stay away from trivia games with them unless, of course, you are on their team. They have three kids, the two oldest of which, Kamala and John, are excellent teachers like their parents. Teachers learn a lot of skills that make for terrific backyard parties. Kamala teaches English and has a talented son named Oliver. John also teaches English and is married to Carly, and they recently have a new son named Zach. Their youngest, Peter, works in the restaurant business in Oakland and is in the music business, a most talented drummer and singer.

The youngest of my husband's sisters, Leslie, is as pretty and sweet as they come. She worked as a sign language translator for TV shows. She is a phenomenal mother with good-looking, adventurous kids (to say the least; daughter Ali with the Peace Corps just returned from Mongolia). We recently attended Ryan's (Ali's twin) wedding: what a gentlemanly, good-looking, talented young man, civil engineer!

Leslie and her husband, Steve, also an engineer, live in LA. Steve is immensely interesting and can throw a long pass.

The second oldest is my guy, Pete, which could explain why he tries to reorganize everything. He is a student forever: gravity, entropy, high-energy physics (Jimmy's field; they argue about at length whenever they see each other, which unfortunately is not often. They even discuss their favorite equations with amazing excitement. What's yours?) and ancient history. He is handsome but doesn't know it or doesn't think it's important. Pete and I live in Walnut Creek, California. Their beautiful, smart, and elegant mother, Shirley, and I became close when she was in a nursing home near my work in Oceanside, California (just north of San Diego). We would drive to the beach and have long and detailed talks, mostly about her varied life experiences and relationships. Then we'd go get fast food for lunch, which she loved. She had a tough upbringing; she loved her dad, but not so much her beautiful mother Olive (they were divorced). An example of Shirley's mother's poor maternal skills, she was a bridge player, and when Shirley came home from school wanting to talk, her mother said, "Shhh" and continued her game. That really bothered Shirley, but after a more chaotic childhood (more stories to go into, but that would be enough to complete this pamphlet), she went on to make something of herself: a deaf teacher, author of *Raising Your Hearing Impaired Child*, 1982, and a terrific mother. I loved her.

Her dad, Barrett Hanawalt, was loved by all his grandchildren. He graduated Stanford in 1913, where he was a gymnast. Barrett remarried a women named Genevieve, known to Pete as Grammy. Every year they rented the same house at Balboa Beach near LA and the family met there (without Pete Sr., who didn't like the beach). Also Gramps and Grammy had great Christmas eve parties at their house in Studio City. After dinner, bells would be heard outside. Gramps would arrive with a Santa hat, a huge string of bells around his shoulders and sack of presents on his back. Pete used to prepare a professional-looking newspaper with family news and send it to his maternal grandfather monthly; I've read many of them and they were hilarious.

XX. PETER'S CHILDREN AND THEIR FAMILIES

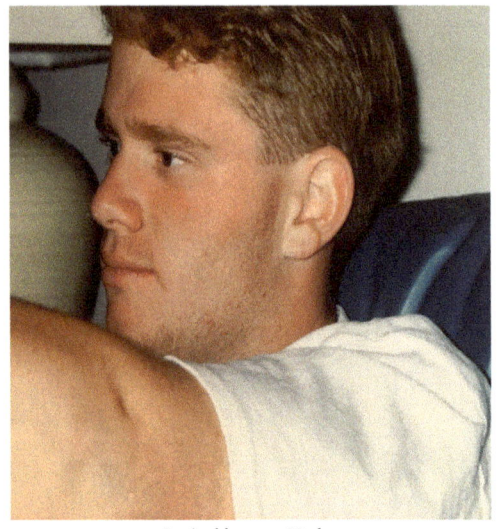

Pete's oldest son, Nathan

When my beloved, Pete, and I got together, he had two wonderful boys. Add that to my three—yep, five. It is interesting that Nate was born exactly one month before the twins. So we have three of our five the same age except one month out of the year. Steve is fourth oldest and Chad the youngest but not by much. You couldn't ask for nicer stepchildren! Nate is so personable and talented. He was the king of his high school class and a star athlete, mostly in football and golf. Nate is fair-haired and fair-skinned, blue-eyed, and sweet and giving. He is a pilot. His talents: a chef, a social director, a therapist, a golfer, a basketball player, pretty much all sports. He can dance too! Chad is a hardworking CPA. He is already a partner in his San Francisco accounting firm. They just moved to a large house in Concord, fifteen miles north of us. Over the years Chad has had many interesting past-times, from ice skating, snow boarding, and off-roading in his fully-equipped Jeep. He is the clever one, full of ideas. He also has a knack for buying the most appropriate gifts. For example, after the maids stole some jewelry from my closet, Chad gave me a dead-bolt lock for my closet. Now who would think of that? He and his cute wife,

Kristina, had a beautiful beach wedding near our boat in San Diego. Kristina grew up near Cleveland, Ohio. Chad has some cousins also in Cleveland, so that's how they met. After a year-long traveling romance, Kristina moved to the Bay Area, and they have given us much joy. The latest is two

beautiful granddaughters. As of this writing, Lauren is six and is always laughing and smiling; she enjoys gymnastics, arts and crafts. Anna is three years old; she is captivating and we are anxious to follow her growth. She is no doubt a smarty with no fear yet; she is very sweet too. You should see her go on her scooter! She loves to explore and climb all over, requiring much oversight. Kristina is the best mother and most efficient employee and wife. They all bless our lives.

XXI. THE FINALE! JIMMY

Yumiko and Jimmy MacNaughton, Japan

Jimmy was such a fast learner at an early age, that it was difficult to keep him challenged. At age 4, for example, he finished all the work-books, advanced for his age, that his mother found for him. So he had an urgent need for additional reading material. Mother and he decided on fairy tales by Hans Christian Andersen, Grimms unabridged version for adults, 300 pages, with very few pictures. Soon he realized these were not based on facts, and it was time to start science and reality.

As he was about to start kindergarten, he was concerned whether the program would be helpful for his future career in science (5 years old!). When he started he asked the teacher to change the program to suit his career goals; teacher of course said no (the teacher was a close friend of mother, so he spoke openly). Frustrated, he decided to fain interest in the activities while actually ignoring them.

In grade school Jimmy already knew he wanted to be a nuclear physicist. While in high school he had decided he wanted to go to UC Berkeley for his PhD in physics. Mother assisted Jimmy with a home learning program, as it was obvious he needed more stimulation than the public school system could provide. In his learning of mathematics, he found that there needed to be trigonometry, even before he knew that it existed and its name.

In his spare time growing up, he played with numbers, such as developing his favorite number, which he often used instead of his name: 2,314,571,011,891,112,685 (*quirk*). He also questioned why our numbering system is based on 10, so he developed and used his own base 12 numbering system with unique symbols (needless to say, he has an amazing memory: other examples are memorizing his credit card numbers; Greyhound bus schedule book; US road maps, etc.).

As you can imagine, Jimmy did very well in high school and college. At Dobyns Bennett High School he did well on tests for gifted students, such as National Merit Scholarship and the Berg Science Plan. He received a partial scholarship for his undergraduate and a full scholarship for his graduate education, as well as some spending money from our parents. He saved much of his allowance and summer job income and put it into a bank account in Kingsport, TN, which exists to this day (*quirk*). Some of this money was used to fund his training at the Monterey, CA, language school. Later, as he travelled and worked extensively in Asia and Europe, he opened bank accounts in many cities.

Besides physics, Jimmy has a passion for learning different languages. It started during school, when he took a Latin course. He became a star student and wondered why they didn't focus on speaking Latin. Through the years he has mastered at least 13 languages. I was in Paris once with Jimmy in 1970 looking for a pair of sunglasses with blue lenses. I had studied French for 3 years but didn't know the word for "lense" so the sales lady was confused. Jimmy came into the shop and told the lady in French exactly what I wanted and I got the sunglasses. Jimmy's language abilities are so good that many natives think he is a local.

Jimmy got his first job postdoc in Nijmegen, the Netherlands. I visited him there, and he showed me around his lab. At that time, German was the international language, so that's what they spoke at work, and their scientific articles and books were written and read in German. Now the international language is English (and the French are really pissed off, as usual; although I agree that French is a beautiful language). One interesting point I noticed: the South in the United States was more judgmental of people who are different; California was more accepting, but there was even a bigger difference between California and Northern Europe. I found the Europeans more mature, well informed about history, politics, and world geography. Jimmy's next job was in Vienna working for CERN. That is where he met his future wife, Yumiko, who was studying piano. Yumiko is incredibly talented musically, petite, nicely dressed, and beautiful; we found later that she is also an excellent tour guide. It is also of note that she came in third in the karaoke contest in all of Japan in 2007. They moved to Japan for autumn, winter, and spring, then back to Austria for the summer. Jimmy still worked in both the Austrian lab and the Japanese lab after he retired. Their biggest challenge was cutting the grass in the Austrian house in the summer. When we visited them in Japan, I decided to prepare for the trip by learning to sing "*La Vie en Rose*," by Edith Piaf. (Why did I pick such a difficult song with my average vocal talent? I guess I want to be French, only because the language is so beautiful…of course, the French can be arrogant, many exceptions noted.) We went to the karaoke bar, which consisted of a computer, a table menu, and songbooks everywhere in many languages. The computer that you sing into judges you on three criteria: rising voice, rhythm, and vibrato (which I don't have). I sang "*La Vie en Rose*" and scored a 70 percent. I did OK on rhythm (my best), not too bad on rising voice, but zero on vibrato. Yumiko sang her songs, and the computer scored her 99 percent every time. She doesn't have a natural vibrato, either, but she waves at her neck, and she does it.

In 2008, Jimmy was on a team of three hundred scientists from thirteen countries that won the Nobel Prize in physics for the Belle experiment. As an aside, Jimmy was the only one who spoke twelve of the thirteen languages; he now knows the thirteenth, Korean. The scientists who led the effort were Kobayashi and Maskawa, who worked at the lab in Tsukuba. They predicted that there is an asymmetry in nature…more matter than antimatter. The experiment found that's there's a difference in the time of decay between meson b-quarks and anti-b-quarks. The matter quarks decayed slightly more slowly.

Comments from Husband, Peter
No story of Margie would be complete without discussing her amazing health triumphs. She was first diagnosed with breast cancer in 2000 and had a successful lumpectomy and chemotherapy. After that she beat the return of breast cancer three more times and was diagnosed with pancreatic cancer in 2007. I'll never forget the worst day of my life while we lived in San Diego, when the endoscopic surgeon pulled me into the hallway and said, "There is a lump in her pancreas, and it is likely cancer." He said, "There is a well-known surgeon at UCSF, or you can have a young, talented surgeon here at Green Hospital, Dr. Jonathan Fisher." We chose Dr. Fisher, and he did a great job in a demanding eight-hour Whipple surgery. All five kids were there and Bob, waiting nervously. Dr. Fisher came out of the operating room visibility drained and told me the operation had gone well. The twenty-five-millimeter tumor was removed along with part

of the head of the pancreas; in addition, the gallbladder, part of the stomach, duodenum, etc., had to be modified and reconnected. The chance of survival without the surgery was maybe 2 two percent (like Steve Jobs), but with the surgery, it was maybe 25 percent. Luckily, the tumor had not metastasized and had smooth fringes. Margie chose to recover on our beloved boat, *TennesSea Breeze*, and we fed her liquid nutrients by tube to her intestines for a few weeks in our tiny floating stateroom, which gave her stomach and organs a chance to heal. As we all know, she endured the recovery well, and we had a five-year-cancer-free party at the Danville house! I had a bunch of United miles collected from all my business trips, and I flew in Nicole from Amsterdam and Mike from Boulder for the party. We blindfolded Margie and all sang verses of "Rocky Top"; after each verse, one of the kids appeared. After all the cancer-free years, unfortunately she now is struggling with Parkinson's. But she has faced it all with great strength and resolve, and her boundless love for her family and extended family and grandkids has kept her very happy.

Announcement

It with great sadness that we lost my cousin, Beth Silver Crawforth, to salivary gland cancer this August 2020 at too young an age. She leaves her husband, Bill Crawforth; her son, T. J., and his wife, Libby; and granddaughters Emersyn and Evelyn. We will always love and miss her.

Acknowledgments

I am indebted to two wonderful, talented people without whom I could never have completed this book, which took much longer than expected. My Parkinson's handicap slowed me down considerably, especially with typing.

First, to my husband of twenty-two years, Peter McArthur, and his constant support with giving me his time, wording, logistics, typing relief, computer support, and by far, his everlasting love.

Second, to Jenny Gonzalez, my part-time caregiver, amazing friend, and superfun companion. She spent weeks on the family tree (her idea), arranging pictures, and typing the manuscript. She is a whiz with her computer abilities. Also a huge thank you to Stephanie Dudley, my current care-giver, who typed some of the revisions and offered wonderful suggestions.

Also to my editors: Thank you for your time, good suggestions, and quick responses. My smart, always-there-for-me daughter, Dr. Nicole Vasilevsky of Portland, Oregon; my talented, generous, and supportive cousin John MacNaughton, of Adrian, Michigan; my smart, always-thinking cousin Ann MacNaughton, of Houston, Texas; my easygoing cousin with impeccable integrity, George McNaughton of Nahant, Massachusetts, and his elegant wife, Deborah, who came up with a most creative idea: she is busy working on a family tree for all of our pets. She seems to have hers fully documented, but as we lived across the street from a rather large valley with, of course, many wild domestic cats, none with papers that I could find, I'll be struggling with this one.

Appendix I

Top right is Archie Curtis, my maternal grandfather, a dairy farmer outside of Alpena. I was told he was the "stud of Alpena County" before he got married. See the resemblance with Margie and her sons. He was born in Blythe, Canada. The other people in the picture are his brothers and sisters.

LOVE, LIFE, QUIRKS, AND QUARKS

The MacNaughton Family: Doug; Bill; their mother, Kathleen; and John. Kingsport, Tennessee.

My aunt Tiz, Uncle John's wife

A FAMILY HISTORY

1972: Margie and Jimmy in Vienna, where Jimmy was working for CERN

*Margie, Phil, and then-wife Vickie on a boat in Galveston
celebrating Aunt Tiz's eighty-fifth birthday*

83

LOVE, LIFE, QUIRKS, AND QUARKS

Ann and Margie's Grandmother MacNaughton, Kathleen, Houston, Texas

My cousin Ann at her wedding in Sausalito with my daughter, Nicole, as flower girl

A FAMILY HISTORY

Front row: Christine, Jim, John. Back row: Peter, Tom, and Margie. Adrian, Michigan.

Jean and Margie, Adrian, Michigan

LOVE, LIFE, QUIRKS, AND QUARKS

Aunt Alice and Uncle Jack's brood. First row: Libby (Beth and Bill's son T. J.'s wife), Carol MacNaughton (Bob's then-wife), Jane Silver, Betsy Silver (Marijean and Don's daughter), Dick's son, Brian, Brian's wife and daughter, Beth, Margie. Back row: Beth and Bill's son T. J.; Bob; Dick; Marijean and Don's son Nick; Don; Dick's son Brian; Cousin Lynn Curtis (more about him later); Beth's husband, Bill Crawforth; Peter. In Dick's backyard, Alpena, Michigan.

Nicole's friend Dayna Sheldon, Nicole, Don, Don's wife, Marijean, at Dick's son Greg and Brook's wedding in the Cascades in western Washington.

A FAMILY HISTORY

Dick and Margie at the wedding

Jane Silver (Dick's wife) and T. J., Beth's son

LOVE, LIFE, QUIRKS, AND QUARKS

Me, brother Bob, Aunt Alice, and Gordon Lynn, in Alpena, Michigan. Dick's backyard, Alice's birthday.

My mother slalom skiing; she had great athletic balance.

A FAMILY HISTORY

Bob loved animals; he and I always had dogs and/ or cats (until I met allergic Pete M.).

My dad. Waterskiing was a big part of our life. Boone Lake, East Tennessee.

LOVE, LIFE, QUIRKS, AND QUARKS

Ex-Peter's mother, Anna, "the Mutterchen," dancing with Michael at Cousin Ann's wedding in Sausalito

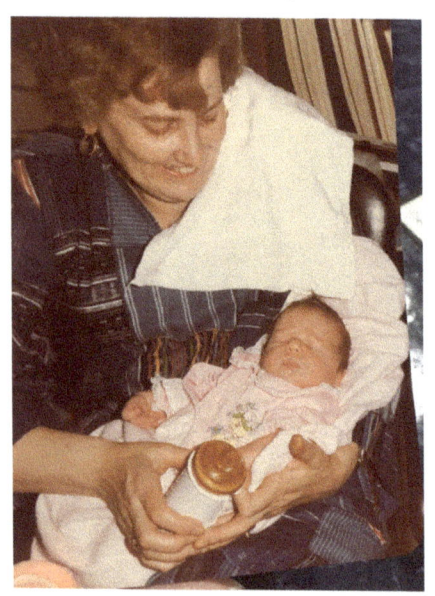

Mutterchen holding Nicole

A FAMILY HISTORY

Ex-Peter's stepfather, Vasyl Klymuk, otherwise known as Dido, and Michael. Michael and Nicole were visiting Dido in New Haven while taking courses at Yale.

Pete's youngest son, Chad. Energetic, inquisitive, traveler, devoted husband and father and a talented accounting executive. Was named partner in his San Francisco firm at age thirty-plus.

LOVE, LIFE, QUIRKS, AND QUARKS

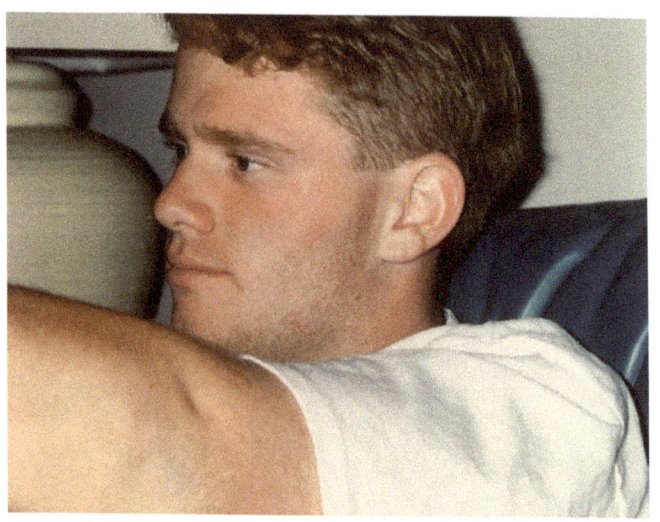

Pete's oldest son, Nathan. A talented sportsman, an incredibly instinctive pilot, promoted to head of multiple flight instructors who were teaching mainly Chinese students who spoke very little English. Loves to cook and sweet stepson!

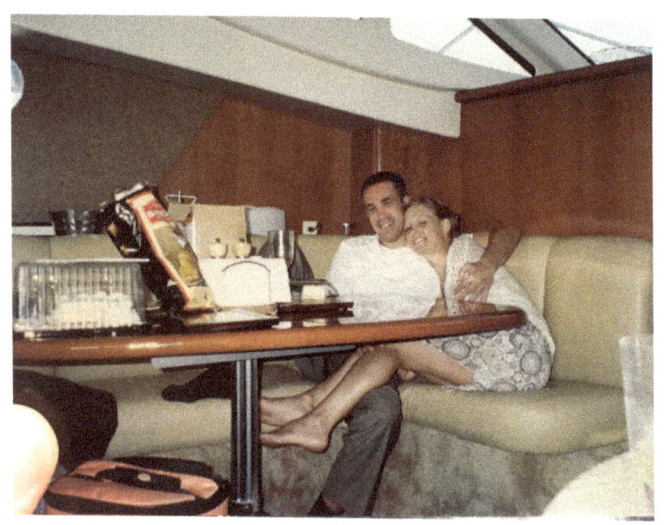

Pete's youngest son, Chad, and his wife, Kristina, on our boat

A FAMILY HISTORY

Our granddaughters: Anna, two, and Lauren, five. Anna is a fearless Energizer bunny. Lauren is fun loving, artistic, and outgoing. Thanks, Chad and Kristina, for the best gift of our lives.

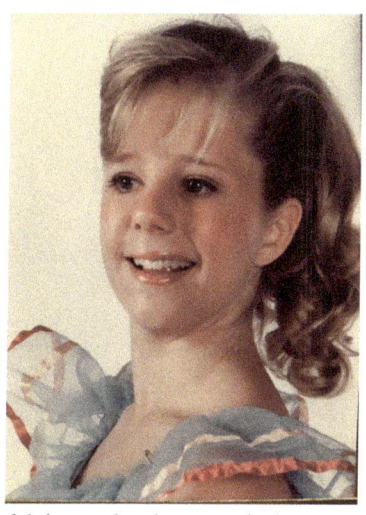

My beautiful dancer daughter, Nicole; loving, enthusiastic, very social like her mom and grandmothers, devoted wife, and a PhD in molecular and cellular biology.

LOVE, LIFE, QUIRKS, AND QUARKS

My oldest son, Michael: Sharp, energetic, independent, a talented musician and pharmaceutical computer application expert, valedictorian of his high school. Studied advanced physics in German in Germany. International traveler. Currently living in Saigon.

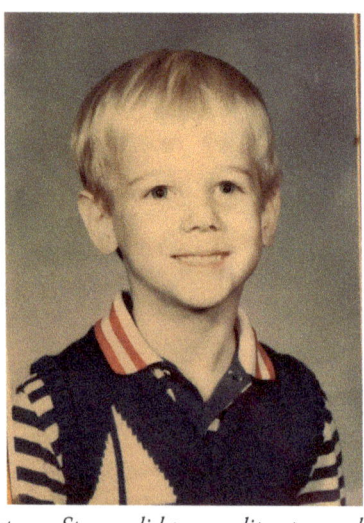

My youngest son, Steve; solid personality, strong physically and mentally, foreign language enthusiast, very talented computer technology expert, and my rock and support system.

A FAMILY HISTORY

Pete and I got married at Post Ranch Inn at Big Sur, one of the most iconic areas on the coast of California; we were so happy that Steve and Chad could attend. The service was conducted by a local woman named Soaring Starkey; Steve gave me away; Chad gave Pete the ring.

Pete and I dancing in our treehouse after the wedding, mostly to the Doors.

LOVE, LIFE, QUIRKS, AND QUARKS

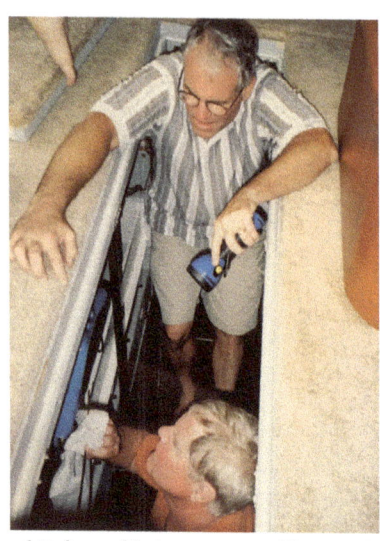

Pete and Bob troubleshooting a problem in the engine compartment of the boat. Happy, happy!

Our treehouse, Innocenti, at Post Ranch Inn, our wedding venue

A FAMILY HISTORY

Spring training for the Oakland A's in Scottsdale with all my kids and Peter

My son Steve, Pete, and Margie at Nicole and Aran's wedding in Portland in 2009

Pete and Margie in Lake Tahoe

Jim and Eileen Loftus, Aran's parents

Aran and Nicole are getting married today!

My brother Bob really loved animals. Here with Steve and the llama that Nicole had at a party at her house in Portland. To my distress, Bob died too young at age sixty-nine due to heart failure.

LOVE, LIFE, QUIRKS, AND QUARKS

Cousin Don Silver and me. We always loved to sing the oldies together. Notice we had similar hair!

With all Pete's and my traveling, we always found time to attend a UT game at Neyland Stadium; it is an amazing atmosphere in Knoxville during football season.

A FAMILY HISTORY

Margie and Dwight Clark, Kona, Hawaii

Brother Bob and girlfriend, Jill, at Long Lake; both were very adventurous.

LOVE, LIFE, QUIRKS, AND QUARKS

Son Mike in front of the house where Aunt Alice, Uncle Gordon, and my mom grew up in Alpena, Michigan

Uncle Doug and Margie, Adrian College

A FAMILY HISTORY

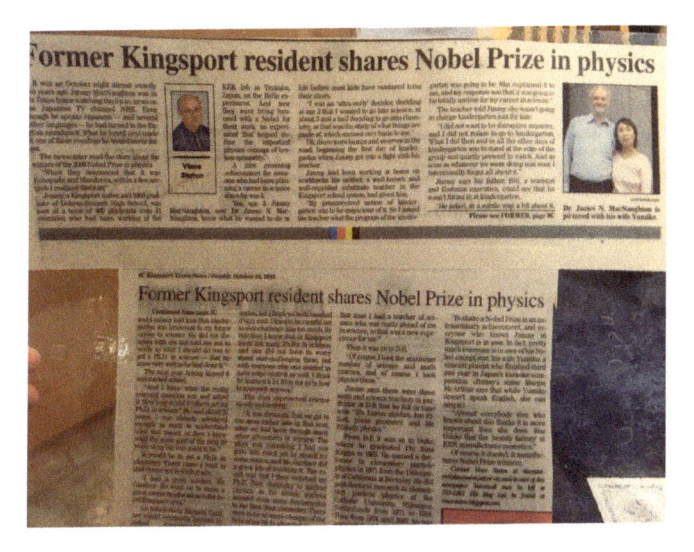

Pete and me horseback riding on Mykonos Island, Greece

LOVE, LIFE, QUIRKS, AND QUARKS

*Peter's great-grandfather, Duncan McArthur.
Without the mustache, see the resemblance?*

Phil and Jeanling in Hawaii

Appendix II

A Couple of Margie's Best Cooking Recipes

Creole Chicken 'n' Dumplings
Serves 6
Seasoning mix:
¾ t. paprika
½ t. white pepper
½ t. onion powder
½ t. garlic powder
½ t. cayenne pepper
½ t. dried thyme leaves

Label a large baggie Creole Seasoning and date. Combine and mix in baggie; I add half to recipe below, but we like spicy. Add less if you want, and store remaining for next time.

Coat 4 chicken half breasts, bone in and skin on, in flour seasoned with two teaspoons of the Creole seasoning. Brown lightly in veg. or olive oil in a large 6-quart pot with a lid on medium heat for about 3 minutes while shaking pot. Turn over chicken, cover pan, remove from heat. Allow to poach without taking lid off for 10 minutes.

Put back on medium heat. Add 2 quarts chicken stock. Add 3 cups each of chopped onions and chopped green peppers (may also add 1 cup chopped celery and 1 cup chopped carrots, if desired). Add 2 cups half-and-half, and add the remaining Creole mix. Bring the mixture to a boil, and simmer for about 30 minutes. Remove the chicken breasts from the pot and when cool enough to handle, remove the skin and remove the white meat and chop into bite-sized pieces. Add the chicken pieces back into the pot and remove from heat.

Make dumplings:
1½ cup flour
1 t. salt
1 t. celery salt
¼ t. baking powder
3 T. melted butter
1 large egg, lightly beaten
4 ½ T. of milk or half-and-half

Mix first four ingredients above in a bowl. Stir in butter, egg, and milk. On a large cutting board, lightly floured, pour out the dumpling dough; knead for 1 minute. Roll out dough about ¼ inch and cut into 1-inch squares. Bring broth to a boil; drop dumplings into broth one at a time. Cover and simmer 20 minutes. (To give it more flavor, you can spoon out about half the veggies, mix in a food processor, and return to broth.) Serve in bowls.

Mutterchen's German Potato Salad
(Goes well with a slab of ham slathered with Dijon mustard and honey, then grilled)
Serves 6
12–18 or so small red potatoes, maybe 1½ inch diameter

Wash and remove any "eyes" (residual roots) from the potatoes. Place in pot large enough to cover all of them with water. Cover with water. Boil until fork tender. It may take 15–30 minutes, but check them with a fork frequently and turn them.

Remove potatoes. Let cool and remove skin (skin should come off with your fingers). Over a bowl, using a knife, cut the potatoes as thinly as you can. Mince at least two shallots; place in a pile in the middle of the potatoes. Add a few twists of salt to shallots. Then add apple cider vinegar to the salted shallots, and let sit for 10 minutes. Then add extra virgin olive oil at a ratio of about 3 parts oil to 1 part vinegar. The amount of vinegar and olive oil is similar to how you would add vinaigrette dressing to a salad.

Serve warm. Delicious!

LOVE, LIFE, QUIRKS, AND QUARKS

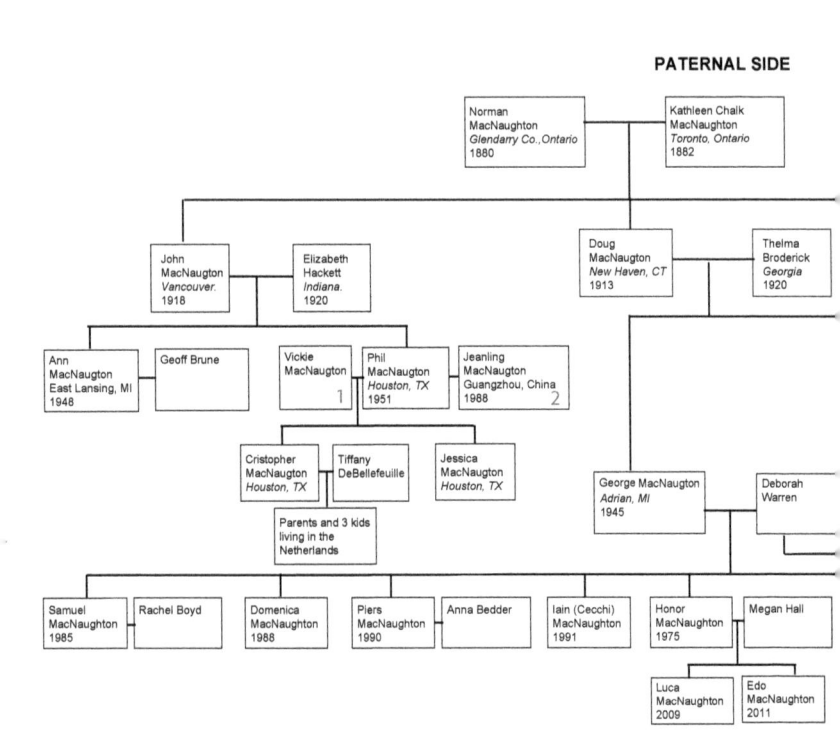

PATERNAL SIDE

- Norman MacNaughton, *Glendarry Co., Ontario*, 1880
- Kathleen Chalk MacNaughton, *Toronto, Ontario*, 1882
  - John MacNaughton, *Vancouver*, 1918
  - Elizabeth Hackett, *Indiana*, 1920
    - Ann MacNaugton, *East Lansing, MI*, 1948
    - Geoff Brune
    - Vickie MacNaughton 1
    - Phil MacNaugton, *Houston, TX*, 1951
    - Jeanling MacNaugton, *Guangzhou, China*, 1988 2
      - Cristopher MacNaughton, *Houston, TX*
      - Tiffany DeBellefeuille
      - Jessica MacNaughton, *Houston, TX*
      - Parents and 3 kids living in the Netherlands
  - Doug MacNaugton, *New Haven, CT*, 1913
  - Thelma Broderick, *Georgia*, 1920
    - George MacNaugton, *Adrian, MI*, 1945
    - Deborah Warren
      - Samuel MacNaughton, 1985
      - Rachel Boyd
      - Domenica MacNaughton, 1988
      - Piers MacNaughton, 1990
      - Anna Bedder
      - Iain (Cecchi) MacNaughton, 1991
      - Honor MacNaughton, 1975
      - Megan Hall
        - Luca MacNaughton, 2009
        - Edo MacNaughton, 2011

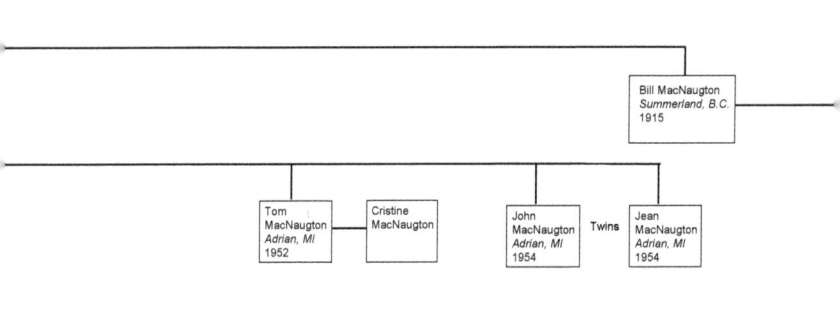

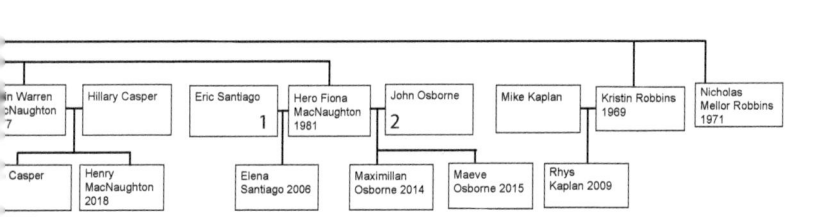

A FAMILY HISTORY

Bill MacNaugton
Summerland, B.C.
1915

Tom MacNaugton
Adrian, MI
1952

Cristine MacNaugton

John MacNaugton
Adrian, MI
1954

Twins

Jean MacNaugton
Adrian, MI
1954

...in Warren cNaughton 7

Hillary Casper

Eric Santiago

Hero Fiona MacNaughton
1981

1

John Osborne

2

Mike Kaplan

Kristin Robbins
1969

Nicholas Mellor Robbins
1971

Casper

Henry MacNaughton
2018

Elena Santiago 2006

Maximillan Osborne 2014

Maeve Osborne 2015

Rhys Kaplan 2009

LOVE, LIFE, QUIRKS, AND QUARKS

MATERNAL SIDE

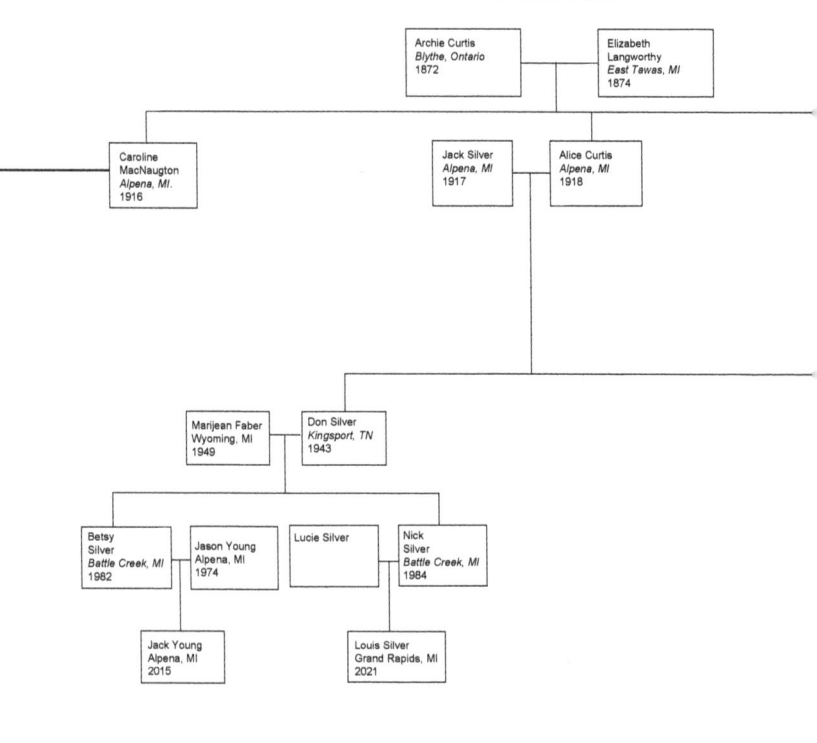

- Archie Curtis, *Blythe, Ontario*, 1872 — Elizabeth Langworthy, *East Tawas, MI*, 1874
  - Caroline MacNaugton, *Alpena, MI*, 1916
  - Jack Silver, *Alpena, MI*, 1917 — Alice Curtis, *Alpena, MI*, 1918
    - Marijean Faber, *Wyoming, MI*, 1949 — Don Silver, *Kingsport, TN*, 1943
      - Betsy Silver, *Battle Creek, MI*, 1982 — Jason Young, *Alpena, MI*, 1974
        - Jack Young, *Alpena, MI*, 2015
      - Lucie Silver — Nick Silver, *Battle Creek, MI*, 1984
        - Louis Silver, *Grand Rapids, MI*, 2021

A FAMILY HISTORY

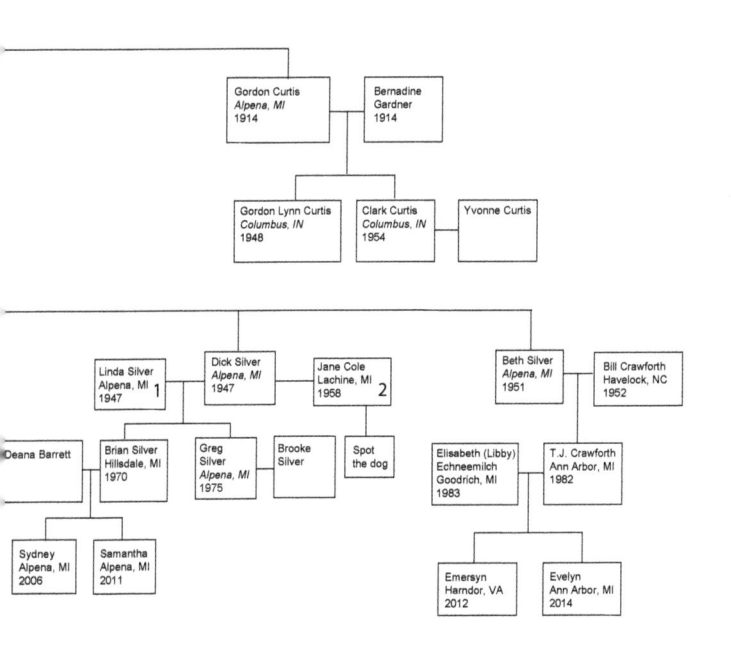

- Gordon Curtis, Alpena, MI, 1914
- Bernadine Gardner, 1914
  - Gordon Lynn Curtis, Columbus, IN, 1948
  - Clark Curtis, Columbus, IN, 1954
  - Yvonne Curtis

- Linda Silver, Alpena, MI, 1947 — 1 — Dick Silver, Alpena, MI, 1947
- Jane Cole, Lachine, MI, 1958 — 2
- Beth Silver, Alpena, MI, 1951 — Bill Crawforth, Havelock, NC, 1952

- Deana Barrett — Brian Silver, Hillsdale, MI, 1970
- Greg Silver, Alpena, MI, 1975
- Brooke Silver
- Spot the dog
- Elisabeth (Libby) Echneemilch, Goodrich, MI, 1983 — T.J. Crawforth, Ann Arbor, MI, 1982

- Sydney, Alpena, MI, 2006
- Samantha, Alpena, MI, 2011
- Emersyn, Harndor, VA, 2012
- Evelyn, Ann Arbor, MI, 2014

111

LOVE, LIFE, QUIRKS, AND QUARKS

MCARTHUR FAMILY

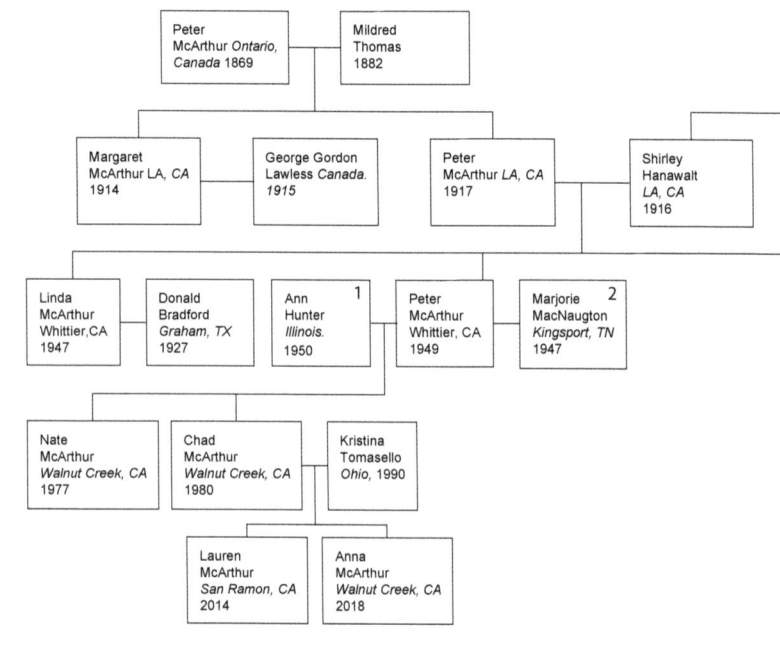

- Peter McArthur *Ontario, Canada* 1869 — Mildred Thomas 1882
  - Margaret McArthur *LA, CA* 1914 — George Gordon Lawless *Canada.* 1915
  - Peter McArthur *LA, CA* 1917 — Shirley Hanawalt *LA, CA* 1916
    - Linda McArthur *Whittier, CA* 1947 — Donald Bradford *Graham, TX* 1927
    - Ann Hunter *Illinois.* 1950 [1] — Peter McArthur *Whittier, CA* 1949 — Marjorie MacNaugton *Kingsport, TN* 1947 [2]
      - Nate McArthur *Walnut Creek, CA* 1977
      - Chad McArthur *Walnut Creek, CA* 1980 — Kristina Tomasello *Ohio,* 1990
        - Lauren McArthur *San Ramon, CA* 2014
        - Anna McArthur *Walnut Creek, CA* 2018

A FAMILY HISTORY

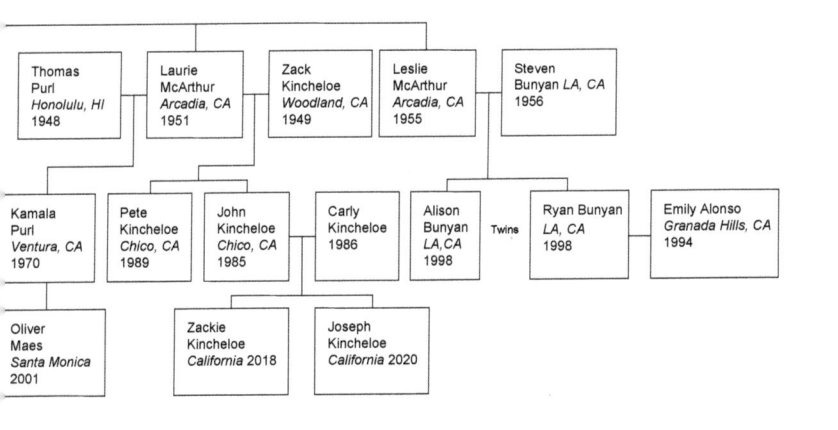

Olive Horn	Barrett Hanawalt
New Hampshire	*Kansas City, MO*
1893	1890

Thomas Purl	Laurie McArthur	Zack Kincheloe	Leslie McArthur	Steven Bunyan
Honolulu, HI	*Arcadia, CA*	*Woodland, CA*	*Arcadia, CA*	*LA, CA*
1948	1951	1949	1955	1956

Kamala Purl	Pete Kincheloe	John Kincheloe	Carly Kincheloe	Alison Bunyan	Ryan Bunyan	Emily Alonso
Ventura, CA	*Chico, CA*	*Chico, CA*		*LA, CA*	*LA, CA*	*Granada Hills, CA*
1970	1989	1985	1986	1998	1998	1994

Twins: Alison Bunyan & Ryan Bunyan

Oliver Maes	Zackie Kincheloe	Joseph Kincheloe
Santa Monica	*California* 2018	*California* 2020
2001		

113

LOVE, LIFE, QUIRKS, AND QUARKS

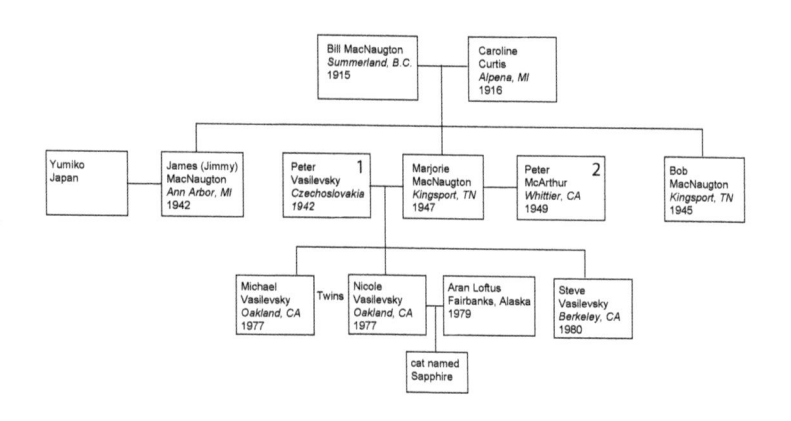

- Bill MacNaugton, *Summerland, B.C.* 1915 — Caroline Curtis, *Alpena, MI* 1916
  - Yumiko, *Japan*
  - James (Jimmy) MacNaugton, *Ann Arbor, MI* 1942
  - Peter Vasilevsky [1], *Czechoslovakia* 1942 — Marjorie MacNaugton, *Kingsport, TN* 1947 — Peter McArthur [2], *Whittier, CA* 1949
    - Michael Vasilevsky, *Oakland, CA* 1977 — Twins — Nicole Vasilevsky, *Oakland, CA* 1977 — Aran Loftus, *Fairbanks, Alaska* 1979
      - cat named Sapphire
    - Steve Vasilevsky, *Berkeley, CA* 1980
  - Bob MacNaugton, *Kingsport, TN* 1945

Lightning Source UK Ltd.
Milton Keynes UK
UKHW021533270821
389531UK00007B/199